U.S. NAVY SEALs

HANS HALBERSTADT

For my good friend Steven Bronson, Chief Petty Officer, United States Navy, Retired,
and a hardcore boat guy in good standing.

The author encourages readers to support the SEALs and SWCC boat crews deployed in service to the United States by
contributing to the following charities:

Naval Special Warfare Foundation, P.O. Box 5365, Virginia Beach, VA 23471

Neil Roberts Memorial Fund, Navy Federal Credit Union, Lynnhaven Branch, 509 Viking Drive, Virginia Beach, VA 23452

First published in 2006 by Zenith Press, an imprint of MBI Publishing Company, 400 First Avenue North, Suite 300, Minneapolis, MN 55401 USA

© 2006, 2011 Zenith Press
Text © 2006, 2011 Hans Halberstadt

Previous edition published 2006. Expanded and updated edition 2011.

Zenith Press titles are also available at discounts in bulk quantity for industrial or sales-promotional use. For details write to Special Sales Manager at MBI Publishing Company, 400 First Avenue North, Suite 300, Minneapolis, MN 55401 USA.

To find out more about our books, visit us online at www.zenithpress.com.

ISBN-13: 978-0-7603-4301-2

The Library of Congress has cataloged the previous edition as follows:

Halberstadt, Hans.
  U.S. Navy SEALs / Halberstadt, Hans.
    p. cm.
  Includes index.
  ISBN-10: 0-7603-2413-1 (pbk.)
  ISBN-13: 978-0-7603-2413-4
  1. United States. Navy. SEALs. I. Title.
VG87.H35 2006
359.984--dc22

                    2006296510

About the author: Hans Halberstadt studied documentary film in college and later took up writing, authoring or co-authoring more than fifty books. Most of his books have been on military subjects, especially U.S. special operations forces, armor, and artillery. He has also written extensively about farming and railroads. Halberstadt served in the U.S. Army as a helicopter door gunner in Vietnam. He and his wife, April, live in San Jose, California.

Unless otherwise noted, all photographs
© Hans Halberstadt/www.militaryphoto.com

Printed in China
10 9 8 7 6 5 4 3 2 1

On the cover: A U.S. Navy SEAL takes up a defensive position in a village in northern Zabul province, Afghanistan, 10 April 2010. *Master Chief Communication Specialist Jeremy L. Wood, Department of Defense*

On the frontispiece: This squad is conducting GOPLATS (gas and oil platforms) take-down drills. GOPLATS in the Persian Gulf are sometimes heavily fortified as well as being inherently dangerous places, loaded with explosive gasses and liquids. They are noisy and have oil-coated decks that make footing uncertain. Real-world GOPLATS take-downs are conducted at night.

On the title page: You won't often see this in daylight, because SEALs cherish the cover of darkness for their run into the beach. Inflatable boats like this one can be launched from submerged submarines or from virtually any kind of ship. The boats can also be dropped from helicopters and C-130s as the SEALs parachute to the surface of the sea.

On the back cover:
The infamous mud flats are one of the memorable joys of Hell Week. They're normally visited on the third night, just as the students think that they've experienced the worst the cadre has to offer. Each one has gone without sleep for seventy-two hours, and everything hurts. Instead of mercy, the cadre pushes them a little harder to see who bends and who breaks under the strain. *Eric Logsdon, U.S. Navy SPECWARCOM*

(bottom left) The caving ladder is a simple tool used by spelunkers. Constructed from thin cable and lightweight aluminum rungs, it rolls into a compact bundle. SEALs find them handy for boarding all sorts of targets, GOPLATS in this case, a mission that uses many of the muscles and teamwork skills acquired at BUD/S.

(bottom right) A SEAL relaxes before his combat rubber raiding craft (CRRC) gets underway.

Contents

Foreword

The SEALs, because of their unique skills, are highly relevant in the war on terrorism. During the first Gulf War, the SEALs really just supported the U.S. Army and Marines. It was a very cautious approach; they did a lot of good work, but in a limited way. The leaders only took on missions that they thought the SEALs could complete successfully and without casualties, partly due to the traditional discomfort conventional commanders have when unconventional forces are assigned to their control. As one of these commanders said of the SEALs during that first Gulf War, "If the SEALs can find a way to use their flippers in the desert, we'll find a mission for them."

That attitude has changed, and SEALs have really come into our own, especially in Afghanistan at places like Tora Bora and elsewhere. SEALs' attitudes have had to change too, and they are learning to do the sort of unconventional warfare and foreign internal defense that army special forces have always done. Naval special warfare (NSW) has done foreign internal defense for years, but now they are doing it better by learning host-nation language skills and cultural issues that SEALs have not had to focus on in the past (although several SEAL teams have been requiring some, but not all, members to have language competencies for years). I think language skills ought to be a requirement for every man on a team, and suspect someday it will be.

The SEALs' traditional emphasis on operations "with one foot in the water" has diminished during the War on Terror mainly because they are very effective at special reconnaissance, direct action missions, and developing their own intelligence information and acting on it immediately. These capabilities aren't limited to the beach—they work just as well in the middle of Afghanistan and the Persian Gulf. The teams like to develop their own intel and run their ops based upon fresh information, something the Green Berets have been doing for decades with the help of indigenous personnel, and the SEALs ought to continue doing more of that in the future.

Sometime in the distant future, I think the teams will get back to concentrating on maritime missions where NSW submarines, submersible vehicles, and combat swimmer training make the SEALs unique within American special operations forces. For the time being, though, there is a need for small units that are very good at responding rapidly and effectively against high-value targets . . . with or without one foot in the water.

—Commander Mark Devine
Navy SEAL Reserve, NavySEALs.com

Acknowledgments

The policy of the U.S. Department of Defense and the U.S. Navy is to release as much information as possible about military institutions and activities while maintaining operational security. That can be a tough compromise sometimes, particularly with communities in special operations. In this case, it means that this book is the product of a close collaboration with the navy, the SEAL community, and individual SEALs. All the photography of active-duty SEALs in this book has been reviewed and approved by both U.S. Naval Special Warfare Command and SEAL Teams Three and Five, who assisted with its production.

Many thanks to the friendly folks at Special Operations Command public affairs at MacDill Air Force Base, Florida, particularly Colonel Jake Dye.

This book wouldn't have been attempted without the reassurance of Rear Admiral Brent Baker, now retired, former Navy

Chief of Information, who responded very graciously to some criticism of mine with an invitation to try working with the Navy again. The result is this book. Sir, I salute you.

Another salute to Lieutenant Commander John Brindley and Journalist First Class Mike Hayden, as hard a pair of public affairs officers as you'll find anywhere, with one of the most difficult missions in the fleet—smack dab in the middle between the media maniacs and the NSW community (whose motto is *No pictures!!! No names!!! No kidding!!!*). To two fine people doing what is usually a thankless job, let me say: Thanks! Well done!

I'd like to personally thank the many folks at BUD/S and SEAL Teams Three and Five who helped so graciously, and against tradition, with this project. I'd like to, but I can't—national security and all. But the Desert Patrol Vehicle guys out at Niland, California, and the squad from Team Five went way out of their way to accommodate a bunch of media weenies and executed their op with a perfect blend of cooperation and consideration.

I *can* thank Rear Admiral Ray Smith—what a guy! He's largely responsible for a new, more open attitude toward public affairs within the NSW community, and it's about time. A salute to you, sir, as well.

Captain Bob Gormly and Commander Gary Stubblefield, both U.S. Navy (ret.), filled in the gaps in my NSW education, shared some wonderful war stories and lots of insights based on long careers in NSW. These are, despite the reputation of the SEALs, gentlemen—the kind of quiet professionals you seldom hear about in this community. It's too bad that more Americans can't know about the things these people and their teams have done for us all.

Thanks also to the current public affairs crew at SPECWAR-COM for assistance with the revised edition—Commandar Jeff Bender, Lieutenant Taylor Clark, Lieutenant (jg) Paul Barrie, Trish O'Connor, and to the superb Photographer's Mate Second Class, Eric Logsdon of the U.S. Navy.

Introduction

Although their numbers are small—there are currently about 2,200 SEALs and about 600 special warfare combatant crewmen (SWCC)—members of the naval special warfare (NSW) community are making a huge impact on enemy forces around the world today. Although most SEAL and SWCC missions never make the news, a few ops have been disclosed.

SEALs conducted many VBSS—visit, board, search, and seizure—missions in the months before the invasion of Iraq, fast-roping from SH-60 helicopters onto the decks of suspect and uncooperative ships. They have had excellent success with oil platform take-downs in the Persian Gulf, and SEALs have conducted hundreds of strategic reconnaissance missions all over Afghanistan and Iraq, slipping into areas where enemy forces are active and then reporting on their activities. Nearly all these missions have been entirely secret except when one goes wrong and SEALs are killed, as happened to Neil Roberts when the CH-47 helicopter he was riding in took heavy fire during an insertion.

SEALs and SWCC are also deployed to South and Central America—at the request of the host nation—to conduct foreign internal defense (FID) in support of counter-drug efforts. Other SEALs and SWCC are just as busy in places like the Philippines, assisting local military units in their efforts to eliminate piracy and prevent terrorist acts by Islamic militants.

This is a busy time for the operators, but it is a busy time for their commanders too, all the way up to the most senior levels of the Department of Defense. There has been a massive shift in the way American forces are organized, trained, equipped, and employed. This change began during the first Gulf War but accelerated afterwards and has had a profound impact on the guys on the SEAL and special boat teams (SBTs). Special operations forces (SOF) has always had an important role, but NSW's ability to respond effectively after 9/11 with the appropriately trained and equipped people for the mission at hand earned the community, and SOF in general, a larger

Above and opposite page: By the late 1960s and early 1970s, the basic gear used by a SEAL for covert insertion by water had evolved a long way from the primitive and extremely basic equipment issued to World War II frogmen. This early SEAL displays a combat swimmer's standard issue—wet suit, fins, face mask, compass board, Draeger rebreather, dive knife, signal flare, and the ever-popular Heckler and Koch MP-5 9mm submachinegun with sound suppressor. *Author's collection*

commanders who did not really know what to do with these unconventional "cowboys." That is radically different today.

While SEAL teams used to be assigned a specific part of the world for their operations, today NSW forces are organized into squadrons and deploy wherever they are needed. There are new boats, new weapons, and lots of new communication systems. NSW career officers are being tasked with some of the most important roles in the War on Terror, with SEAL officers assigned to roles where they make policy rather than execute it.

A SEAL, Rear Admiral Albert Calland III, commanded the first forces fighting in Afghanistan, and a Green Beret, Colonel Cleveland, controlled all American forces in Northern Iraq during the invasion of March and April 2003. One result of this is that SOF from all the services are getting more missions than in the past, and more critical missions too. At the time of this writing, Marine Corps Force Recon teams were working with NSW, providing support for SEALs while at the same time conducting their own traditional missions.

As this role shifted in the early 1990s, it became obvious that more SEALs and SWCC were going to be needed. Several new SEAL teams have been created, and recruiting for both SEALs and SBTs have been intensified. The nature of the training has changed as well; basic underwater demolition/SEALS (BUD/S) is just as demanding as ever, and the attrition rate remains huge. But the guys on the SEAL teams and the guys on the boats are now integrated on the same team during their pre-deployment workup in a way that is comparatively new.

That is especially true when NSW squadrons deploy and come under the tactical control of a combined or joint special operations task force. Then a SEAL platoon (or several platoons) is teamed up with a Mk V boat detachment, several special operations craft–riverine (SOC-R) boats and their crews, and their intel teams and other supporting players. They will serve alongside Operational Detachment Alphas, the standard twelve-man Green Beret A-team.

When SEALs and SWCC are working closely with the army's special forces, it is sometimes difficult to tell them apart—they're both operating far inland and both conducting the same sort of missions. Both avoid wearing distinctive insignia or uniforms, but you can still make a good guess. If a guy on the battlefield is wearing a ball cap instead of a Kevlar helmet and is loaded to the gills with weapons, and has longish hair, he's likely to be in one of the SOF commands.

role in America's defense strategy. Under Secretary of Defense Donald Rumsfeld, U.S. Special Operations Command (USSOCOM) has been given unprecedented authority to prosecute the Global War on Terror, including the largest budget increase in its history as well as the ability, if so ordered, to direct operations in any theater and be supported by the regional commander—as opposed to supplying forces to support the theater commander.

In the past, Green Berets, SEALs, Rangers, and the other members of the SOF, were "chopped," or assigned to theater

9

Chapter 1

LET SLIP THE FROGS OF WAR

An essential part of NSW are the unsung heroes, the special boat squadrons (SBSs) and their assortment of heavily armed boats. The boat guys share much of the danger, discomfort, and adrenalin, but without all the public acclaim. SEALs, however, are usually careful to give them credit for their critical role in accomplishing the mission.

Naval special warfare (NSW) has been a very important and much abused subject for more than sixty years. For the U.S. Navy it goes back to the Underwater Demolition Teams of World War II, who cleared beach obstacles and surveyed gradients for amphibious landings in the Pacific and against European shores, many dying in the attempt. It is an extremely dangerous set of missions that cannot be practically executed with other, less demanding means.

The organization and the people of the NSW are actually two communities, one being the men *in* the water, the Sea/Air/Land commandos (SEALs), and the other being the men *on* the water, the special boat squadrons (SBS). Both have a long and distinguished combat record, and both communities have been linked together as NSW for more than forty years. While the SEALs get most of the attention and notoriety, SBS crews have been doing a lot of the shooting and bleeding over the years. While most of the SBS crews are not graduates of the basic underwater demolition/SEALs (BUD/s) training program the boat officers are SEALs, and SBS personnel are held to the same high standard of performance as the more notorious part of the team. This story is about both.

The men in NSW are just one part of a big, broad spectrum of American combat power—in fact, a tiny slice of the pie. There are only about 2,000 of them in the U.S. Navy, far fewer than the U.S. Army's 7,000 or so Green Berets (active and reserve). SEALs, along with the U.S. Army's Ranger regiment and Green Berets, comprise the United States' most elite surface combat operations resources. All are masters of basic infantry tactics; each has its own area of expertise. All train together at some points of their qualification. All, despite their parentage as components of the Navy or Army, are really on-call assets for the highest levels of the national command authority (NCA)— the president, the secretary of defense, and the Joint Chiefs of Staff. When they go to war, their mission will probably start at MacDill Air Force Base, Florida, where U.S. Special Operations Command (SOCOM) is headquartered. It is that kind of organization: powerful, dangerous, expensive, and above all, *special*. There is also something traditionally a bit odd about these special forces soldiers and sailors. They are isolated and aloof from the rest of the military and especially from the public, partly by design and partly by tradition.

The great virtue of NSW is the ability to execute military missions anywhere on the globe, particularly on the world's oceans. Here a SEAL team clambers up the side of a ship, something they can do without warning, even in the middle of the Pacific, even in the middle of the night.

The process of preparing for SEAL missions never ends. When a team returns from one deployment, they begin the process of refreshing their skills for the next. And among the skills that must be the freshest are those involved in close quarters battle, or CQB. Here an instructor reminds SEALs of the fundamentals associated with the M4 carbine. *Eric Logsdon, U.S. Navy SPECWARCOM*

The Big Picture: SOCOM

SOCOM is one of the best funded, most secure, most competitive parts of the U.S. force structure. All the services, including the Coast Guard, have been caught up, to some extent, in the post–Cold War reorientation away from "high-intensity combat," with its need for nuclear weapons, long-range bombers, numerous tank divisions and aircraft carriers, to "low-intensity combat," where combatants are harder to identify, therefore requiring the work of small teams of extremely adept people like SEALs and Green Berets.

SOCOM is just one of eight unified commands within the U.S. armed forces and has been a major player in the defenses of America since 1987. It integrates assets from all the services into one organization with one commander and with the same basic set of missions for everybody. That doesn't mean that everybody does the same thing; rather it means that the navy, army, and air force pool their talents and resources for planning, training, and executing missions. The navy's contribution to SOCOM is

NSW command, comprised of SEAL teams, special boat squadrons, and swimmer delivery vehicle teams.

Special operations forces have traditionally been the "bad boys" of all the services. Many senior officers have, over the years, been candid about their loathing of the "cowboys" within their large, conservative organizations. Special forces training and missions produce a kind of lunatic intensity that is accepted within these groups but that clashes badly with the larger navy or army community within which it is supposed to function. Special operators have a reputation (well earned by an earlier generation) of using their own independent criteria for acceptable behavior. Green Berets used to say, when asked if they were in the army, "No, I'm in special forces." Some still do.

Becoming a SEAL or a Green Beret has never, as a result, been considered the fast track to high rank. It was, and still is, a special place for special men (and, very rarely and not in the SEALs, a few incredible women) who consider these extremely demanding roles a kind of calling. They aren't in the business to

SEALs never operate alone and every man has a buddy to watch his back and to haul his carcass back to the beach if necessary. The buddy team concept begins in BUD/S and lasts as long as a man is on a team. The fundamental building block of SEAL missions is the swim pair.

Above and opposite: The foundation of NSW is based on the combat swimmer skills developed by the UDT frogmen of World War II. They remain important today for covert insertions on targets near the water.

get rich or famous but to be measured by the highest standard of military performance and found acceptable. That is the real lure and the real reward of the special forces.

While the special operators may not always be personally popular within their services, the additional stress and funding for such missions has made for a very competitive budgetary environment. Both the Army and the Marine Corps compete with the Navy for the missions carried out by the SEALs. In fact, you could stand on a beach being infiltrated by combat swimmers and be very hard pressed to know who was about to kill you—U.S. Army Green Berets or Rangers, Marine Corps Force Recon, or U.S. Navy SEALs. All use precisely the same weapons, boats, dive gear, radios, and uniforms—and all train for what sometimes looks like the same exact mission. But it turns out that the missions do have distinctions and the overlap is not as great as it initially appears.

Joint Special Operations Command

Joint Special Operations Command (JSOC) is a kind of planning and coordination cell, headquartered at Pope Air Force Base, North Carolina, (co-located with Fort Bragg). It was created in 1980 as a joint headquarters designated to study the techniques and requirements of all the Special Operation Forces (SOF) components, including NSW—in other words, to ensure that everybody's playing off the same sheet of music.

NSW Development Group (NSWDG), formerly known as "SEAL Team Six," is one of two units under JSOC—along with Delta Force—that are so secret the Department of Defense does not acknowledge their existence. NSWDG is responsible for counterterrorist operations in maritime environments and is one of only a few U.S. military units authorized to conduct preemptive action against suspected terrorists and terrorist facilities.

SEAL Specialties

In contrast with air force and army special operators in the ranger regiment and special forces groups, SEALs are generalists, although each will have a specialty—intelligence, submarine operations, weapons, engineering, communications—that he does in support of the organization in the planning process. But once the squad of SEALs goes off to war, he has to be able to do the job of anybody else on the team. "If I'm the platoon commander on a mission and I take a hit," one SEAL officer says, "the assistant platoon commander can take over. It doesn't matter if he was the corpsman or the radioman, he can take over that operation and direct it to completion. I can pick up the radio, treat a wound, use any of the weapons. Green Berets say they can do that too, but I think we build generalists while they build specialists. That's probably because they operate in larger groups. We operate in groups anywhere from four to sixteen men, and any one of our guys can slip into the role of any other guy . . . within limitations."

SEAL Missions

Just about all the special operations forces have the same basic list of missions. Each of them adapts these missions to the unique talents of the force. For the NSW community the list looks like this:

1. Direct action (DA)—Short-term seize, destroy, damage, or capture operations. Attacks against facilities ashore or afloat; prisoner snatch operations; small offensive combat operations against hostile forces.

2. Special reconnaissance (SR)—Reconnaissance and surveillance operations. Covert beach surveys, listening posts, observation posts.

3. Unconventional warfare (UW)—Training, leading, and equipping partisan and guerrilla forces, behind enemy lines.

4. Foreign internal defense (FID)—Training, advising, and teaching the military, paramilitary, and law enforcement personnel of allied nations. Professional development, normally in a noncombat environment.

5. Counterterrorist operations (CT)—Operations conducted against terrorist units and individuals. May be as direct responses to terrorist operations or as indirect, preventive, deterrence measures.

All these missions have implications for their missionaries. To accomplish missions like these and survive, the people and the organizations they belong to need to be agile (individually and organizationally), trained to a far higher standard than conventional military personnel, and provided with far more resources, man for man, than conventional units. This assignment makes for organizations that are expensive and exclusive.

The "Wiring Diagram"

Special warfare command (SPECWARCOM) is an interesting community. Although the SEAL teams are its most famous component, they are only one part of the whole business of NSW—a fairly small part, in fact.

A rear admiral commands two major combat resources, NSW Groups One and Two. Each of these groups is organized into:

Three SEAL teams, comprised of eight 16-man platoons, which conduct reconnaissance, DA, UW, FID, and other operations in maritime or riverine environments

One SEAL delivery vehicle (SDV) team which operates and maintains submersible systems that deliver and recover SEALs in hostile areas and conduct reconnaissance and DA missions

NSW units, which are small command and control elements located outside the continental United States, support other NSW forces assigned to theater special operations commands (SOCs) or components of naval task forces.

Group One—assigned SEAL teams One, Three, and Five—operates out of Coronado, California, and generally deploys forces to the Pacific and the Persian Gulf. Group Two—with teams Two, Four, and Eight—is headquartered at Little Creek, Virginia, and is responsible for operations in and around the Atlantic, including Europe and Latin America. These two headquarters are the administrative foundations for special warfare and, despite the sneers from the operators in the field about the "puzzle palace" (as such headquarters are often called) they are essential to the efficient coordination of assets and activities.

Coronado is not only home to NSW and Group One, but also to the notorious NSW Center where SEALs are trained. Basic underwater demolition/SEAL (BUD/S) training is conducted at Coronado, the entry point for all new SEALs and SEAL delivery team members. The center also conducts advanced training and professional development programs for members of the SPECWARCOM community.

Little Creek, besides hosting Group Two, is responsible for the Special Warfare Development Group. This is the SEAL think tank where new weapons, tactics, communication systems, and dive equipment are tested, evaluated, and written into doctrine. Little Creek is also responsible for the development of special operations tactics for air, ground, and maritime forces, in and out of NSW. SPECWARCOM includes detachments in Alaska and Hawaii, plus five special warfare units.

What you don't see advertised are the semi-covert programs called Development Group and Red Cell. Development Group provides support for a variety of classified programs that—sorry—we aren't going to tell you about. Red Cell is an offshoot from the Naval Security Coordination Team and has the interesting mission of assisting navy commands around the world with their security problems. This help is not always welcomed because it is done in a sneaky way when the Red Cell members sneak or break into what are supposed to be secure facilities. They are supposed to act like terrorists or subversives—and that's the way a lot of people outside NSW think of them. Some commanders seem to think Red Cell creates more security problems than it solves. This program was at one time extremely notorious and the subject of a book by one of its former commanders (written while in prison) that scandalized NSW. It appears at this writing that the program will be transferred out of NSW into the more conventional naval investigative service.

SEAL and Special Boat Squadron Basics

Although we usually refer to this community as SEALs, it is a bigger, more complicated business than the SEALs alone. The other major part of SPECWARCOM is the guys on the surface who go through the same training at BUD/S, go off on the same missions, and bleed at least as much as the members of the SEAL teams—the special boat squadrons (SBS) and the members of the special warfare units. They're all NSW members, although all the attention and glory seems to go to the SEALs alone. But, as the history of NSW in Vietnam and after shows, much of the combat and the killing has been done by the riverine warriors duking it out with the bad guys ashore with .50-caliber machine guns and Mk 19 grenade launchers, all while roaring around in their PBRs (patrol boats, river) in a nonstealthy way.

The idea behind the boat squadrons is to provide the SEAL teams with dedicated, organic mobility, as well as some kinds of

teams with dedicated, organic mobility, as well as some kinds of special patrol and surface strike missions. These squadrons are commanded by SEALs but manned largely by sailors from the surface warfare community, what SEALs often call the "black shoe" navy. Although part of the NSW community, they are not quite SEALs but rather SEAL support units.

The home base for SEAL/SBS operations seems somehow out of place on the luxurious, tropical paradise of Coronado, California, just across the bay from San Diego. While tanned tourists frolic on the beach nearby, SEAL/SBS operations and training are planned and conducted at the Naval SPECWARCOM, a component of U.S. Special Warfare Command. The headquarters is just another rather modern concrete building, complete with the requisite lawn and landscaping, plus plenty of chain-link fence, guards, and razor wire.

The U.S. Navy takes the prize for inventing and actually using the world's biggest and most awkward acronyms, one of

which is SPECWARCOM. You might as well get used to words like this because everybody in the SEAL/SBS community uses them all the time; they are unavoidable. SPECWARCOM is the parent headquarters for all navy special operations of which SEALs are only a part.

SEAL Teams

On paper at least, a full-up SEAL team includes ten platoons of SEALs plus a small support staff from the black shoe navy. This support staff are the yeomen for administrative support, radiomen, ordnance specialists, a navy diver to help with the dive locker—about twenty non-SEAL personnel. There is an additional command element including the commanding officer, executive officer, and operations officer, all of whom are SEAL-qualified.

While in theory there are ten platoons in each team, it doesn't usually work out that neatly. Each team has an intense

available to participate in a platoon. But each of the platoons will have sixteen SEALs assigned: two officers and fourteen enlisted members. These are grouped further into two squads of eight, each getting an officer and seven enlisted. The squads themselves are split into fire teams of four men, the fire teams each having two swim pairs.

The squad has traditionally been the organization of choice for SEAL operations and has turned out to be a very efficient group for many missions.

A lot of SEAL equipment is designed around these groups. The Mk V patrol boat is designed to accommodate sixteen SEALs. Fire teams of four fully-combat-loaded SEALs fit very nicely into a combat rubber raiding craft. The patrol craft, Mk I is designed to carry a squad of eight SEALs.

SEAL Mobile Training Teams

SEALs (and Green Berets) are deployed all over the world, all the time; not just in high-profile places like Afghanistan and Iraq, but also on quiet little assignments that you never read about in the papers—even while dramatic things happen and the proverbial poop hits that fabled propeller. These deploy-

The tail gunner provides rear security for a squad moving across an open beach in daylight. He's carrying an M60E3 medium machine gun, a variant of the weapon that has been in service for more then thirty years and is gradually being replaced by the M48 on the teams.

(SBS-26), forward based out of Rodman in Panama but with people and boats busy in many Latin American nations.

These organizations, along with SEAL Team Four, are tasked with providing mobile training teams (MTTs) to Bolivia, Argentina, Brazil, Colombia, Equador, and other nations where drugs are manufactured. All these countries have extensive river systems; there are more than 140,000 miles of navigable rivers in South America, with 20,000 in Bolivia alone. These become the highways for transportation of drugs. To control the drug flow requires efficient, effective patrol of the rivers, something the SBS folks do better than anybody.

The MTTs involve quite small numbers of U.S. personnel and equipment to train rather large numbers of host-nation personnel. Sometimes the SEAL/SBS team doesn't even supply the boats. Once on scene the SBS team starts working with the boat operators from the host nation while the SEALs work with the police or military people who will do the patrolling ashore. In Bolivia this force is called the Blue Devils; it has been almost entirely trained by these MTTs. The SBS and SEAL dets have helped the Bolivians develop four bases for counter-drug operations deep in the jungle.

In Colombia the story is a little different. The U.S. Marine Corps runs the show there, where they've had a long and chummy relationship with the Colombian marines. The Colombian det includes one officer and four enlisted SEAL/SBS personnel, all with a special interest in riverine operations and with Spanish language skills. MTTs in Colombia, as elsewhere in the program, last six months.

Special Warfare Units and Forward Basing

Since there are so few SEALs to go around, and since the "real world" has a way of blowing up in your face unexpectedly, NSW has developed forward bases closer to the potential hot spots of the

ments have two functions: one is to put the special forces people out near the scene of a possible crime, before it is committed, ready to respond; the other is to train in environments a lot more realistic than are available in the United States.

One of these quiet deployments ("dets" in the trade jargon) nobody ever hears about—especially with all the higher profile post-9/11 operations that have taken place—is in support of the anti-drug war in Central and South America. Although U.S. law prohibits SEAL/SBSs and other American military personnel from active combat, U.S. policy is to use special operations forces personnel to train the trigger pullers to a high standard. And executing that mission is the team of Naval Special Warfare Unit Eight (NSWU-8) and Special Boat Squadron Twenty-Six

world" has a way of blowing up in your face unexpectedly, NSW has developed forward bases closer to the potential hot spots of the world than Coronado or Little Creek. These are the NSW units (NSWUs), each with people, facilities, and equipment intended to speed up the process of planning and launching missions.

There are five NSWUs. When the real world starts acting up these are reorganized as NSW task groups and units and start manning up with extra personnel from in and out of the NSW community. An emergency will probably find assets getting requisitioned from other NSWUs, particularly the exotic, complex swimmer delivery vehicle (SDV), which may be flown in from the United States.

Two SWUs serve the European Command area from bases in Spain and Scotland. The NSWU base in Spain (NSWU-

6) uses rigid inflatable boats (RIBs), patrol boats, coastal (PBCs), and Mk V patrol boats. The base in Scotland (NSWU-2) uses RIBs only. The Pacific Command is served by NSWU-1, recently repositioned from the Philippines to Guam; like NSWU-6, it uses RIBs, PCs, and Mk V patrol boats. NSWU-8 serves the extremely busy Southern Command out of Rodman Naval Station in Panama, supporting the busy counternarcotics operations with a mix of riverine and coastal patrol boats and the RIBs. Detachments in Hawaii and Alaska provide SEALs with a broad range of training options.

Besides these forward bases, two large NSW groups on the East and West coasts of the United States provide a continental United States (CONUS) foundation for operations "downrange."

One of the things that has changed tremendously for SEALS and all American tactical operators over the past ten years is the kind of combat equipment or "battle rattle" worn on missions. The SEALs in this 1992 photograph all wear the old standard web gear with suspenders, pistol belt, ammunition pouches, and canteens, that changed very little from the Vietnam era until about 1995. Modern systems are based on a modular vest pattern and often include ballistic armor plates.

For some NSW assets, forward basing is the only practical way to show up on time for the little "come as you are" wars that are the stock in trade of special operations forces. The PCs, for example, are far too big to go anywhere except under their own power. Although they are fast, it's a mighty big world. If they had to self-deploy from the United States, it could take these ships almost three weeks to arrive at some possible operational areas.

Change of Mission

The commander's intent for American special operations has changed quite a bit since the idea was first used fifty years ago, at the outset of World War II. Back then, the idea was to provide support for partisans and guerrillas in occupied France, Yugoslavia, China, and elsewhere. It involved very little—if

any—direct combat. It was a training, leading, and supplying role for forces that tried their best to avoid direct contact with German or Japanese forces while collecting intelligence and sabotaging vehicles, railroads, and bridges, and occasionally assassinating an individual enemy.

Special operations forces today still train for that mission—and SEALs execute something like it every day—in nations all over the world. The trainees aren't guerrillas anymore, but soldiers, sailors, and law enforcement officers from nations such as Colombia, Bolivia, and Kuwait; and the enemy is now quite often the guerrilla-like forces who manufacture and distribute drugs or terrorists in Ireland, the Middle East, or Latin America.

The War on Terror has, more than anything else, inspired much of the mission of today's SEALs and other SOF communities. The tasking for NSW is now, essentially, to be prepared to conduct short-notice small-unit operations at night over the horizon, to infiltrate from sea, air, or land in adverse weather. Instead of training others to fight large, conventional battles, SOF units, including the SEALs, are much more like global SWAT teams that can be sent to fight almost anybody, almost anywhere. Like a good SWAT team, these forces are task-organized and are based on stealth, shock, surprise, and precision. While some SEALs still study foreign languages and are charismatic instructors for people of extremely alien cultures, the heavy emphasis now is on preparing SEALs to be able to slither deep into hostile territory up to easy pistol range of very specific bad guys, put 9mm bullets between their eyes, and get out without being obvious about it. The battlefield can be a hotel, an airliner, a civilian cargo ship, an oil platform, a factory, or an embassy. And the enemy may be one hostile man—or woman—surrounded by innocents.

This is a tall order. In fact, it is sometimes too tall; SEALs aren't, despite what you hear, supermen. They get tapped to do impossible missions sometimes because they are so skilled, so sneaky, so confident . . . and they die in the attempt, sometimes, as in Panama and Grenada, when they're pushed beyond their

Chapter 2

A SHORT HISTORY LESSON

This motley crew is a squad of warrior SEALs from long ago and far away. Standing are Pierre Birtz, Bill Garnett, Charlie Bump, and Bob Gormly; kneeling are Jess Tollison and Fred McCarty; the photo was taken in 1967. With Gormly (then a lieutenant) as squad leader, these men operated around the town of Binh Thuy, helping establish the reputation of the SEALs as among the most elite American warriors. All made naval special warfare a profession, and all are now retired except for Tollison, who was killed in an accident at the Niland, California, training facility in 1971. Gormly went on to command SEAL Teams Two and Six, UDT-12, and NSW Group Two before retiring in 1992 as a captain. *Bob Gormly collection*

The keel for today's SEALs and special boat squadrons (SBSs) was laid in May 1942 with the formation of the naval combat demolition unit at Fort Pierce, Florida. The men who were selected for the program came from the naval construction battalions and the U.S. Navy/Marine Corps Scout and Raider volunteers. All had extensive swim experience; some were commercial divers; all were in superb physical condition. The training was not too different, fifty years ago, from today—lots of physical training (PT), lots of swimming, lots of demolitions. The stress level was high, by design. Training continued day and night, in the swamps with the alligators, on the beaches, and offshore.

The motivation for the program had come toward the end of the previous year. After less than a year of war, the United States was beginning to strike back at the entrenched Japanese, first at Guadalcanal, then, in November, at Tarawa... "terrible Tarawa," as it will always be known to the Marine Corps.

The United States was badly unprepared for war, and even more unprepared for large-scale, long-range amphibious operations. One thing that makes war interesting is the way individuals and nations respond to the surprises and stresses imposed on them by events. In the case of the U.S. Navy and Marine Corps in 1942, this meant not merely the attack of Japanese installations in the Pacific, but the seizure of critical bases.

Many of the basic frogman techniques in use today were invented half a century ago in the pressure cooker of war. That includes the technique for deploying a line of swimmers off an enemy-held beach from a high-speed boat.

Guadalcanal came first, and the invasion phase of the operation, at least, was a cakewalk. The marines were able to step ashore, essentially unopposed, often with dry feet. Getting the force ashore was just the least of the problems at Guadalcanal, most of which came soon thereafter. The navy had been lucky with that phase of the operation. Tarawa was different. D-day for Tarawa was 20 November 1942. Information about the island, its defenses, and its approaches was limited. Hydrographic data was sketchy, tidal data almost nonexistent. The assault force commander took a risk, knowing the stakes, and lost.

The marines were sent in aboard conventional landing craft. Five hundred yards offshore, within the range of Japanese machine guns, the boats ground to a halt against coral reefs. The marines, in the grand tradition, jumped off the boat ramps for the long wade into the beach . . . and died in droves. Many stepped into depressions in the coral reef; heavily loaded, they sank and drowned. The rest had to endure the heavy, interlocking fields of fire from the Japanese defenders. It was a disaster.

Hundreds of marines died before the battle for Tarawa really even began. In a way, their lives were wasted, but in another way, by dying this way, they taught the navy a lesson. The lesson was, and still is, that amphibious assaults are high-risk operations that require careful preparation. And that need for battlefield preparation was the idea for the development of the navy combat demolition unit.

The unit's mission was to scout possible invasion beaches and to clear, with explosives, obstacles that might prevent the invasion force from reaching the beach, as had happened at Tarawa. It was recognized that there were essentially four hazards to the force: enemy action from fortifications ashore, enemy-built obstacles such as concrete blocks placed in the water, natural obstacles such as the coral reef that stopped the marines, and the time and range of the tides.

That was the program for the sturdy volunteers at Fort Pierce. The survivors of the challenging training were organized as small units, structured with six enlisted men and one officer per combat demolition unit and shipped off to England with the rest of the American contingent building up for the invasion of France.

When finally, on 6 June 1944, Allied forces were ready to take Europe back from the Nazis, the first men ashore were the navy combat demolition teams (NCDTs). The NCDT members were tasked with the nasty chore of surveying and destroying the beach obstacles emplaced by the Germans along the Normandy coast of France. These obstacles were an ingenious and extensive array of concrete blocks, steel spikes, mines, and barbed wire that cluttered most of the beaches suitable for amphibious landings. Left in place, they certainly would deter any large force from putting men ashore. And in 1943 the Germans knew the Allies were going to come, sooner or later, and were working as fast as possible to make a beach passage as costly as possible.

When the Allies finally struck, the NCDT men were out in front of the first wave. With the most primitive equipment, utterly lacking effective protection from the chilly water, they swam in to the beach in the small hours before the invasion. Working from one massive obstacle to the next, hanging satchel charges linked with detonation cord, they prepared to clear the beaches for the assault elements.

Dawn that day found an incredible armada off the Normandy coast—thousands of ships and boats finally bringing hundreds of thousands of soldiers back to Europe—and the beaches still hadn't been completely cleared. The NCDT men had been given a tall order, and not all the obstacles had been blown by the time the infantry started in to the beach. As the cloudy sky brightened, German gunners could see, and engage, the men setting charges on the beach whose mission was obvious. While the NCDT men struggled frantically to avoid the fire, emplace the explosives, and blow the lanes for the landing craft, the first wave closed on the beaches.

Even without clear access to some of the beaches, the craft disgorged their cargoes of infantry when and where they could, often under intense artillery and heavy machine gun fire. The NCDT men worked as fast as they could, but even so they found infantry sheltering behind obstacles rigged and primed for demolition, despite warning devices. Some charges blew with infantry nearby, killing them, while other obstacles weren't blown because of the proximity of men from the first wave.

Even so, four lanes were cleared and the assault elements generally made it ashore—if not in good order, at least in one piece, one infantry division after another. The cost for the NCDT force was far higher than for the infantry—about 30 percent at Utah Beach, about 65 percent at Omaha, about 40 percent casualties overall. But, from the point of view of the planners, that was a small price to pay for getting a secure foothold on the heavily defended enemy shore.

Despite the losses and the problems the NCDT units encountered, their work was considered a success and adapted to the island-hopping campaign in the Pacific. They were rechristened underwater demolition teams (UDT), each with a hundred enlisted men and thirteen officers assigned, and retaining the seven-man unit foundation.

February 1969. A SEAL ties a block of C4 into a line of det cord before placing the charge in a Viet Cong (VC) tunnel complex. Vietnam honed the special warfare abilities of the little SEAL community to a sharp edge through an emphasis on small-unit independent operations that made individual platoons and squads responsible for "taking care of business."

"Hey! You said the mud wasn't deep!" The op hasn't even started and this guy is already out of action—up to his knees in mud. The weapon is the infamous Stoner, a 5.56mm machine gun with a tendency to jam at embarrassing moments. When it worked, though, it could chew up whatever it was pointed at, and the idea behind it survives today in the light-weight version of the M60 still used by the squads.

Out in the Pacific the UDT units developed a routine that became part of the standard operating procedure (SOP) for amphibious assaults, some of which survives to the present day. This routine started with a beach reconnaissance four days before the scheduled assault (D-minus-4) with the swimmers inserted just at first or last light. This recon would identify obstacles, natural and man-made, on the intended lanes for the landing craft and armored amphibious tractors (AAM-TRACs), recording each carefully and developing a chart of the offshore, nearshore, foreshore, backshore, and hinterland areas of the invasion beaches.

On D-minus-1 or on D-day itself the obstacles would be blown. The method developed fifty years ago is still taught today because it still works. Here's how they did it:

While naval gunfire and close air support aircraft light up the beach with guns, bombs, rockets, and cannon fire, a small, fast ship makes a high-speed run into the beach. During World War II, modified destroyer-escorts were used and designated attack personnel destroyers (APDs). Several miles offshore the APDs stopped and lowered four LCPR landing craft, each with a rubber duck lashed to the port side. These LCPRs then made a high-speed splash run parallel to the beach, about a thousand meters out, starboard side facing the shore. One after another the swimmers rolled out of the LCPR into the rubber duck and, on command, into the water, forming a line of swimmers. At a thousand meters the small portion of each man's head is essentially invisible, and while the defenders might possibly have spotted one with powerful binoculars, the aerial bombardment and naval gunfire tended to make them worry about other issues.

The men swam ashore and executed their missions, either a reconnaissance or a beach clearance, then withdrew back to the thousand-meter line offshore for pickup, again forming a line of swimmers at intervals. The LCPR came zooming up the line again, with a rubber sling extended. By forming a crook with his right arm and kicking hard just before the boat came by, the swimmer could come up partially out of the water and snag the sling rigged from the inflatable boat, to then be smoothly plucked from the ocean slingshot fashion. One after another the line of swimmers could be quickly and (under the circumstances) safely recovered.

The actual demolition of the beach obstacles also became something of an art form, still practiced today. That technique sent swimmers in to assigned obstacles with satchel charges essentially identical to the ones used today. The flank swimmers at either end of the line carried long rolls of "det cord" instead of explosives; while the other swimmers were busy installing the satchel charges, the det cord was strung from one end of the beach to the other. The satchel charges were each tied into this det cord, and then most of the swimmers began to withdraw. Finally, the ends of the det cord were double-primed, once from each end, with a blasting cap and time fuse. Using waterproof fuse lighters, the fuse was lit, and the whole team formed up out at the thousand-meter line for pickup. When either of the fuses finally burned down to its blasting cap, the powder train was initiated; the det cord linked all the charges and caused all to go off within a small fraction of a second—hopefully when the swimmers were already well offshore and safe from the blast effect and chunks of concrete and steel that rained down after such a mission. After Normandy, UDT losses dropped to only about 1 percent from the approximately 40 percent of the first large-scale operation, thanks largely to this technique. By the end of the war, thirty-four teams, including about 3,500 officers and men, were in action in the Pacific.

Korea

In the grand American military tradition, much of the equipment and experience of the UDTs in World War II was discarded promptly after VJ-day—only to be reinvented a few years later. For UDT that came in September 1950 with the audacious amphibious landing at Inchon, Korea.

With United Nations (UN) forces trapped in a shrinking perimeter at the southern tip of Korea by a rampaging, nearly victorious North Korean army, General Douglas MacArthur and his staff designed an "end run" operation on the enemy, with the port city of Inchon on the western coast of the peninsula, near the already fallen capital of Seoul, as the target.

The harbor at Inchon is a treacherous one, with an extreme range of tides that would make the timing and execution of any amphibious operation extremely critical. To minimize the danger, UDT was used to provide detailed information about channels, docks, tides, and defenses. They cleared channels of mines the hard way, by hand, swimming in line-abreast and attaching charges to the mines as they were encountered.

After the Inchon invasion totally changed the complexion of the war, with the North Koreans reeling back, the UDT units were used again, but not just for beach recons and clearance missions. Their skill and experience earned them assignments to blow bridges, railroads, tunnels, and similar targets well away from the beaches.

From a thousand feet overhead, the farms and rivers of Mekong Delta look deceptively tranquil in this pre-op recon photo. Within the lush growth along the river are likely to be bunkers and fighting positions. Inland, among the fields and groves, may lurk more enemy facilities and stores—and the enemy himself. *Gary Stubbenfield*

Korea was the first of a series of nasty little wars that didn't conform to the expectations of the strategic planners in Washington, but that didn't prevent soldiers, sailors, and marines from having to fight them. Korea didn't really fit what the American public expected, either, and consequently support for the war and the men fighting it slowly ebbed a bit until the stalemate was formalized with a truce in 1953. But Korea expanded the mission of the organization that would soon be rechristened "SEALs" and included guerrilla operations behind the lines, parachute jumps, and other missions quite different from those envisioned ten years previously during the bigger conflict of World War II. And more was yet to come.

The Vietnam War

Although the ancestors of the units and the missions that would become the navy's and army's special operations forces existed during World War II, it was not until 1962 that they achieved real recognition and support. The support came from President John

F. Kennedy, a student of international conflict and unconventional warfare. Kennedy had read the works of Mao Tse Tung and Che Guevara, and he understood the changing nature of conflict away from nuclear confrontation to brush-fire wars. While the United States was reasonably well prepared for the former, he knew better than many of his generals and admirals how badly the United States was prepared for unconventional warfare.

Kennedy was aware of the British success against guerrillas in Malaysia in the late 1950s. The Brits turned the guerrilla's tactics and strategies around on them, learning to live in the jungle where they fought and winning uncounted little battles. Kennedy perceived a warning and an opportunity. As a newly elected president, he was in a position to make things happen, and he did. He didn't invent the SEALs or the Green Berets; both organizations already existed but were allowed meager resources and roles.

The army, in particular, loathed the fledgling special operations units that existed at the time. They refused to play fair in exercises and frequently disrupted the intended outcome. As a result, wearing the green beret was a court-martial offense at Fort Bragg—until Kennedy showed up. The navy wasn't as parochial, but the UDTs were still hardly a barnacle on the chain of command.

Kennedy put the whole Department of Defense on notice that there was about to be a change of mission. The change was from a focus on a northern European, NATO-versus-Warsaw Pact conflict, to the kinds of wars Kennedy thought the United States was likely to actually have to fight. He said, "This is another type of warfare, new in its intensity, ancient in its art—war by guerrillas, subversives, insurgents, assassins—war by ambush, instead of by combat—war by infiltration instead of aggression; seeking victory by eroding and exhausting the enemy instead of engaging him. And these are the kinds of challenges that will be before us in the next decade, if freedom is to be saved—a whole new kind of strategy, a wholly different kind of force, and therefore a new and wholly different kind of military training."

Kennedy insisted not only on new training, new organization, and new strategies, but on new weapons and equipment as well. He was responsible for the development and introduction of the AR15/M16 rifle and the jungle boot, with its steel insert to protect against punji stakes. But it was the development of what became known as a *special warfare* capability within the U.S. Department of Defense that was one of Kennedy's most inspired and enduring legacies.

The army's special forces (known popularly but unofficially as the Green Berets) and the navy's SEALs and SBSs share many things, including missions, heritage, and a strong sense of mutual respect. Both were developed, at Kennedy's insistence, in the early 1960s. At the outset, both were envisioned as extensions of the World War II Office of Strategic Services (OSS) teams that

A patrol boat, river (PBR) noses into the shoreline to de-bus a squad of SEALs. Swift, stealthy, surprising ops in the Mekong delta essentially turned guerrilla warfare around on the VC and NVA, keeping them off balance and insecure. It was accomplished by a skillful combination of boat crews and SEAL teams, operating together in a way that still makes sense. *U.S. Navy*

After calling for help, the squad runs off the mountain—right through this tiny pass. Overhead are the NVA, momentarily distracted by Cobra gunships firing up their positions. The squad, expecting a shower of enemy grenades at any moment, is on the run. Lieutenant Bob Gormly leads the way, followed by Clay Grady and Ed Bowen, none of whom are too thrilled about the op. *Bob Gormly collection*

One and Two, assigned to the Pacific and Atlantic theaters. The original mission was to conduct NSW, which then meant unconventional warfare, counterguerrilla, and clandestine operations in maritime and riverine environments. This meant, theoretically, the capability to destroy enemy shipping and harbor facilities; infiltrate and extract friendly force agents, guerrillas, and escapees; conduct reconnaissance and surveillance; conduct counterinsurgency civic action; and organize, train, and lead paramilitary forces.

The new organization got its first taste of real world operations shortly thereafter, conducting operations in support of the Cuban Missile Crisis in 1962, and again in 1965 in the Dominican Republic. Neither lasted long or received much attention, but both put the teams under the kind of pressure that only happens during genuine hostilities. It was a useful rehearsal for the big war that was about to begin. SEALs in small numbers shipped out to Vietnam in 1962, working out of Da Nang and functioning in an advisory role to the Vietnamese navy, much as the Green Berets were doing for the of Vietnamese army at the same time.

SEAL Team One trained up and deployed two platoons to Vietnam in 1965, assigned to operate in the Rung Sat Special Zone near the capital city of Saigon. These platoons started operating in areas never previously visited by American or Vietnamese forces, deep in the mazes of rivers, creeks, and channels where the communist South Vietnamese rebels, or Viet Cong (VC), had been safe. The platoons set up listening posts to collect information on VC activity and ambushes to turn the VC activity off.

The poor VC would come cruising back from a night on the town, shooting up the nearest government outpost, collecting "taxes" from farmers going to market, or assassinating mayors or other officials who might be friendly to Saigon, putting along a deserted stretch of canal in their sampans on the way back to base all fat, dumb, and happy. Then, suddenly, the canal bank would erupt as machine guns and rifles opened up from an

parachuted behind enemy lines to train, equip, lead, and inspire the native population, a catalyst that used a few men to put hundreds of soldiers in the field. It was called *unconventional warfare* and it was a good idea. It worked—in some times and in some places.

Birth of the SEALs and SBSs

The SEALs were officially born on 1 January 1962, with President Kennedy doing the honors, commissioning Teams

artfully prepared ambush. The VC were either killed or captured, their operational routine disrupted, and their influence over the local population severely reduced. The American SEALs were turning a VC tactic around and using it effectively. It just wasn't fair, somehow! It was stealthy, sneaky, and utterly unexpected—just what Americans were not supposed to be able to do, setting the tone for the conduct of NSW to the present day.

The results from this preliminary experiment were quite successful, and four additional platoons were soon sent, two assigned to Nha Be, one to Binh Thuy, and another to My Tho. With a headquarters element, Detachment Alpha, set up at Subic Bay in the Philippines, the SEALs were ready to lock and load. Detachment Bravo went aboard an APD as a component of a beach recon group, Detachment Charlie went aboard two fleet submarines (the USS *Perch* and USS *Tunney*), and Detachment Delta was sent to Da Nang, Republic of Vietnam. Detachments Echo and Foxtrot went aboard the amphibious ready group standing off the coast, with assignments to assist with demolitions and beach surveys. But it was Dets Golf and Hotel, the riverine patrols, that most frequently closed with the enemy and where much of the legend of the SEALs in that war was built.

SEALs were again deployed to Vietnam in 1966, first to the area around Saigon and later to the rich, heavily populated Mekong Delta. The platoons did their workup together, deployed together, and returned together after six-month tours. This made for a kind of intimacy and unit cohesion far stronger than the main force army units in the country at the time, where soldiers rotated in and out of units individually for one-year tours.

In some important ways, the lessons of the SEAL platoons and teams during the war in Vietnam have been ignored and overlooked. Within the limited areas in which they operated, these little units became highly effective in a generally ineffective war. Their efforts were independent of a larger strategy and so failed to have a lasting impact on the bigger campaign, but they did show what could—and still can—be done by extremely small, stealthy units operating in a maritime environment.

The platoons were given tremendous freedom to conduct their operations as they saw fit. They developed their own intelligence, plans, and procedures, and executed their missions pretty much without interference or support from the army or air force or from the local Vietnamese military commanders.

Although they avoided working with the local Army of the Republic of Vietnam (ARVN) as much as possible, the SEAL teams often included Vietnamese SEALs. Some of these men were very good; they provided excellent translation services and often exhibited a high degree of combat discipline.

The most common and appropriate use of the SEAL teams were in ambushes, recon missions, and prisoner snatches. The small size of the units, even when supported with gunboats and ground-support aircraft, normally kept the platoons from engaging anything bigger than an enemy platoon or, if it couldn't be avoided, a company or even a battalion. Their flexibility and experience, the effective and efficient support from the boat units, and the air and intelligence teams attached to the SEAL platoons all made for a successful fighting force and a style of operations that is extremely different than that used today.

In the Mekong Delta, particularly, SEAL operations ranged from simple ambushes to complex joint operations, staged from navy ships located over the horizon, involving transit to the beach in small craft. SEALs used army helicopter gunships, naval gunfire support, U.S. Air Force fast-movers, and army helicopters again, this time the slicks for extraction from hot landing zones. SEALs also ran the provincial reconnaissance units (PRUs) as part of the exotic Phoenix program.

Platoons at the time used fourteen men, but a typical mission usually called for no more than seven. Intelligence collection for an operation usually took several weeks and was developed concurrently with other operations. The platoon leader would design a mission around resources and objectives. Helicopters would be laid on for gunship fire support, the boats would be scheduled, an interpreter and a Vietnamese SEAL assigned. The helo crews were briefed, the squads received a warning order, and then, when the plan was fully refined, they got an operation order. Gary Stubblefield, a retired SEAL commander, says, "Briefings in those days took one hour, an hour and a half, max. We already knew our SOPs, we already knew our area. All we had to do was catch up with the changes required for the specific mission. The hard part was the 'actions at the objective' portion, where we got really detailed.

"Typically, we'd leave some time after dark, insert sometime before midnight, maintain an ambush until about daylight, break the ambush, and get back in the boats to go back to the base."

A War Story

Captain Bob Gormly has commanded SEAL Teams Two and Six, UDT-12, and NSW Group Two during a long career in NSW, just concluded. As a young lieutenant he went to Vietnam with SEAL Team Two's first deployment to the combat zone in 1967. SEAL Team Two was sent to the Mekong Delta, a hotbed of enemy activity, in the first use of the SEALs in that part of the country—though Team One had been working for some time up to the north, around Saigon.

"Our operations at first were kind of 'touch and feel,'" he says. "We were always searching for a strategy that we fitted into—and we never found it—but we had a lot of fun. Us young lieutenants had tremendous freedom about how we wanted to run an operation. We couldn't be told by anybody to run an operation that we didn't want to do."

Back then the entire delta was considered "Indian" country—hostile territory. The only real U.S. presence was the Navy River Patrol Force (CTF-116), which used PBRs to patrol the major rivers for about a year, getting shot at regularly. The VC had pretty much free run of the rest of the area.

The problem for the newly established SEALs from Team Two was first to find out what was going on. That required an intelligence information program, something that began immediately with requests for overflights, interrogations of prisoners, radio intercepts, and similar information-gathering techniques.

Gormly developed his own little plan for how he wanted to operate. First, the SEALs wouldn't go where other friendly forces could operate—there probably wouldn't be anything there, and it made coordination with friendly forces more efficient.

After considering the available intelligence information—the intel, as it's called—Gormly would call for a navy Seawolf helicopter and go for a ride. He flew over the area he was interested in to get a sense of the lay of the land, looking for signs of enemy activity. Although there were no U.S. forces in the area, other than CTF-116, there were a few trustworthy American officers in the delta who could help keep the chaos and confusion to a minimum.

"Then I'd land at the subsector headquarters to meet with the senior U.S. advisor, usually a U.S. Army captain or major, who would be working with the local Vietnamese provincial and subsector commanders. I'd walk in and tell him, 'Hi, I'm Bob Gormly. I've got a SEAL team, and we want to operate in your subsector—and I don't want anybody else to know about it but *you*.' To a man, they all agreed to that condition. Then I'd tell them, 'I'm going to be out there sometime in the next three or four days. I'm not going to tell you when. Just, please, don't put H&I [harassment and interdiction artillery fire] in there.'

"Then I'd go back to base, get the platoon together, start running whatever intel we had on the place, setting up to go. We usually went the next night.

"Just before we launched, within six hours, I sent a UNODIR [unless otherwise directed] message . . . a *flash* message that went to all higher headquarters that began 'Unless Otherwise Directed,' and indicated where we were going. Never once was I told not to go. Then we'd hop in the boat and head down river.

"We traveled very light, only small arms, plus an M60 machine gun and an M79 grenade launcher. The briefing was simple; I made sure everybody had the equipment they were assigned, then I told them where we were going, when, and what we were going to do. 'Any questions? No? Let's go!'

"We jumped in the boat, a twenty-two-foot trimaran and took off. The boat was a seventy-five-mile-per-hour boat that we made into a twenty-five-mile-per-hour boat by adding a lot of weight in the form of ceramic armor, weapons, and a lot of people."

The SOP for ambushes involved cruising down one of the main rivers or canals into the general area of the objective, inserting several kilometers ("klicks," in the trade), and walking in to the ambush site along another canal. A typical mission involved a boat trip of fifty kilometers or so up the lazy river, as fast as possible for most of the trip, then as quietly and innocently as possible for the last few klicks. Navigation in the confused maze of canals was a tremendous problem, generally one the skipper of the boat was responsible for. If he was good you arrived where you planned to go—if not, you could have a real problem.

The most dangerous and vulnerable concern was the problem of getting off the boat and into the local woodwork without being noticed. Nearly all insertions were done in the middle of the night. Rather than run the boat up into the weeds and debark the patrol in obvious fashion, the insertion was usually conducted in a more sneaky way. While the boat motored along in normal fashion, the team members merely stepped off the stern in patrol order, swam ashore, and slithered up on the bank. They all waited silently for ten minutes or so, listening for any movement that might indicate they'd been compromised and that enemy forces were moving in to investigate. If that happened, the boat could be recalled for an emergency extraction. Otherwise the mission proceeded according to SOP and to plan.

In the delta, the patrol moved out into the rice paddies, staying off the dikes and away from the treelines where enemy soldiers were most likely to be. Movement was extremely slow and careful, the SEALs moving quietly toward the intended ambush site, normally a canal bank, usually several klicks from the insertion point.

"Although we were in a free-fire zone where everything that moved at night was considered enemy," Gormly says, "we were more selective. Unless I actually saw weapons on the boats we would call the boat over to the bank and search it. If they were 'clean' I'd just take the sampan down the canal a ways and hold them there while we waited for somebody else to come along. One night we had to wait for four sampans before one came along that belonged to the bad guys."

SOP for that kind of contact was for the patrol leader to initiate the ambush, typically at quite short range where the M60, the M16s on full-auto, and the M79 grenade launcher's focused fire shredded the wooden vessel and its crew. The team would wait for the leader to fire, sometimes with full-tracers, the signal to "hose down" the enemy vessel. "Seven guys carry a *lot* of firepower," Gormly recalls. "If it was a good hit and there were a lot of weapons aboard we might stick around to see what happened—

Members of a SEAL team are put ashore utilizing a navy landing craft (LCM), to begin a mission in the Rung Sat Special zone of South Vietnam. Trained to conduct unconventional or para-military operations, each SEAL is a qualified parachutist, a former underwater demolition team (UDT) member, proficient in at least one foreign language, and an expert in all types of hand-to-hand combat and self-defense measures.

maybe somebody would come over to investigate. Then we could ambush them too!"

After the patrol leader was satisfied with the evening's mayhem, the order to move was given. The detained boats were released, much to the relief of the fishermen aboard, and the SEALs would move off toward the extraction point. The pickup boat was already somewhere in the vicinity for the scheduled recovery of the team, waiting for a radio call. The team was recovered and headed back to base for debriefing and chow. In a couple of days it would be time for another briefing and another mission.

This pattern was used for the vast majority of SEAL missions of all types, including recons and prisoner snatches, with slight variations. Recons involved insertion around two or three in the morning, then patrolling into a predetermined overwatch location, setting up a "hide," and staying very still all day. Air or artillery fire

could be called in on targets of opportunity. Finally, late at night, the SEALs patroled back out to be extracted.

While this was a pretty efficient way of running operations, it was hardly without risk. Gormly was asked to send a team onto Cu Lao Tan Dinh, an island in the delta where enemy gunners routinely shot up passing patrol boats from fortified bunker complexes. With several patrol boats standing by for fire support, the team inserted at first light on 7 June 1967, loaded with hundreds of pounds of C4 explosive, blasting caps, detonation cord, and fuse.

Once ashore, Gormly's motley crew "sneaked and peeked" finding lots of bunkers in the process but not encountering any of the loyal opposing team. With the patrol boat supplying the demo materials, the team methodically blew up every bunker in sight. They did this for about four hours, moving steadily down

Chapter 3

EARNING YOUR FLIPPERS AT BUD/S

A visit to the infamous mud flats is one of the memorable joys of Hell Week. *Eric Logsdon, U.S. Navy SPECWARCOM*

Opposite page: Climbing the cargo net is harder than it looks; it squirms and sways with the movement of the men negotiating it. The instructors demand each student go as fast as he can—or faster. But the real challenge comes at the top, when you have to scramble over the log and get a good grip before heading back down. With your arms seemingly on fire from the long climb, it is easy to loose your grip while trying to make a hasty transition from one side to the other. Students fall from this and other stations on the O course and some are seriously injured. *Eric Logsdon, U.S. Navy SPECWARCOM*

So you think you wanna be a SEAL? No problem—piece of cake. Anybody can do it! It only takes twenty-six weeks, and the training is mostly done on the beautiful, sandy beach at Coronado, California, right on the Pacific Ocean near warm, wonderful San Diego, and the program is run by a large, kind, attentive, cheerful, and well-trained staff of SEALs. There are always plenty of beautiful women strolling by to admire the handsome sailors; the famous and luxurious Hotel Del Coronado, with its superb restaurants and bars, is right down the road. There is plenty of sailing, surfing, scuba diving, and other recreation available in the immediate vicinity. The beach is always available for a nice jog. And, best of all, every instructor at the BUD/S program is committed to making sure that every day of those twenty-six weeks are just loaded with

Once a BUD/S student gets through the first phase of training, the job skills become part of the program. These four Phase II students are preparing for a surface swim in the frigid Pacific. All students discover on Day One how cold the water is, but by this part of BUD/S, they have the comparative luxury of a wet suit for protection against hypothermia. *Eric Logsdon, U.S. Navy SPECWARCOM*

activities and experiences you will never forget. Sound like fun? Sign right here!

Well, Navy recruiters don't actually sell prospective recruits that rosy view of the program. But despite many cautions, SEAL candidates often show up at BUD/S without a realistic understanding of what is actually involved in the training required to earn the Budweiser trident emblem of a SEAL. The truth is that it is one of the most difficult, challenging, and actually brutal learning experiences anybody can have, and one of the things most people learn is that they don't really want to be a SEAL quite badly enough to finish the program.

Like the army's Green Beret qualification course (or Q Course), BUD/S is a *selection* and training program that weeds out people who don't belong—that usually means most of them. They are weeded out the only way that anybody has ever found for reliably selecting people who can hack the problem—by cranking up the stress so high that only the strongest survive and the quitters quit—or break. It is not nice and it isn't pretty. There isn't any other way. And sometimes it results in nearly every member of an entering class of SEAL candidates being eliminated. In one class *not one* single man graduated. It is a calculatedly brutal experience that is not pretty to watch and

pushes its victims to their limits of physical and emotional endurance, and beyond. Injuries are routine and deaths in training occasionally occur.

But, in a way, it is true that anybody can survive it—if they have the appropriate state of mind. It takes plenty of strength, but most of it isn't muscular; it's mental. If you've got the mental strength to work through the discomfort, the fatigue, and the humiliation, you can probably develop the physical strength, SEALs tell you. The head is the hard part. And no other test has, so far, been able to figure out how to find the men who won't quit from those who will without pushing them both far beyond the normal limits of civilized routine.

The BUD/S training takes twenty-six weeks, but it is only one part of the process of becoming a fully qualified SEAL. Before even applying for training a prospective candidate must pass the very strict physical examination for navy divers; have eyesight at least 20/40 in one eye and 20/70 in the other, correctable to 20/20, without color blindness; score high on military written tests; be male and twenty-eight years of age or less; and pass the physical fitness test. Extremely high scores are expected on the fitness test, which includes a five-hundred-yard swim (breast or side stroke) in less than twelve

Above and right: On the third night of Hell Week, students begin to think it can't get any worse and that they've experienced the worst evolutions the cadre have to offer. Their feet are getting raw, each one has gone without sleep for seventy-two hours, and everything hurts. Instead of mercy, the cadre pushes them all a little harder and deeper into their misery in an effort to see who breaks and who bends under the strain. Some guys will quit here. It is bad; it will get worse. *Eric Logsdon, U.S. Navy SPECWARCOM*

and a half minutes (followed by a ten minute rest), forty-two push-ups in two minutes, at least fifty sit-ups in two minutes, eight pull-ups, and a mile-and-a-half run in boots and BDU pants in under eleven and a half minutes—all totaling less than an hour.

Applicants must come from certain navy ratings, have the endorsement of their commanders, and have plenty of time remaining on

their enlistment. If you fit all these requirements you can apply, and you might even be accepted and assigned a slot in a class. If that happens, don't wait to start your physical conditioning program. You don't go to BUD/S to get in shape; you *arrive* in shape, or you will fail almost instantly. "In order to even apply," Rear Admiral Ray Smith says, "you've got to be a top-notch sailor. We've got the pick of the guys coming out of the Naval Academy, more enlisted applicants than we can handle."

Although the published standards call for a cutoff age of twenty-eight, older men are sometimes accepted, and some are

even recruited. Two thirty-six-year-olds have completed the program, and at least one man was thirty-two at the time. While the older bodies are a little less resilient sometimes, that can be offset by greater maturity and better self-discipline. One of these, a Polish refugee with extensive language skills, a former teacher and, at the time, a competitive gymnast, was recruited for the program and made it through training on the first try.

New arrivals will indeed see the marvelous Hotel Del Coronado, the pretty sailboats, the girls sunbathing on the beach, and the glittering Pacific Ocean and will soon learn that the Pacific is freezing, that the beach is for running on and rolling in, that the girls and the tourist attractions exist only as torture devices.

For seven long weeks the trainees endure a program of indoctrination and physical preconditioning, with long hours of classes, running, swimming, sit-ups, pushups, calisthenics. They sweat and struggle . . . but they still haven't started BUD/S yet.

The Only Easy Day Was Yesterday

Phase One of BUD/S is the basic physical and mental conditioning portion of the program. It lasts nine weeks. It features a lot of running, swimming, and trips around the obstacle course. Every trainee is required to put his maximum effort into every test, every time. The minimum scores are raised each week. Each trainee is required to improve on his previous scores. Instructors

watch and evaluate every hopeful trainee like hawks—or vultures—ready to pounce on any flaw or failure, real or imagined. It is an extremely abrasive, competitive process. The only way the instructors will leave you alone is if you've just beaten everybody else at an event; then you might be allowed a few minutes to gloat and relax while the rest of the class thrashes around in the surf zone.

This continues for five weeks. Each day the heat is turned up a little more. The instructors push harder and harder; they never let up for a moment. As they say over and over, "The only easy day was *yesterday!*"

The students spend lots of time in the water, and the water is cold, even in summer. Hypothermia is a fact of life and occasional death. Wet suits are sometimes used, sometimes not; even with the suits, the cold Pacific Ocean seeps in, lowering body temperature. Students can be seen shivering violently some-

Previous page and above: Despite five days with almost no sleep, the last morning of Hell Week will keep anybody awake. The cadre make sure of that by firing M60 machine guns and artillery simulators while the students who haven't quit yet crawl around on the ground while being yelled at. There is no fixed time when it all stops; that is up to the commander and the staff. This student is within an hour or two of the order to suspend Hell Week festivities. *Eric Logsdon, U.S. Navy SPECWARCOM*

The low crawl under the wire is always a popular event on the O course and is one of the easier stations, except when you have to go through it on your back, like this.

"Get wet and sandy!" is the command, and off the students dash to the surf for a quick dip in the chilly ocean. Then they run back to the berm where each must roll around enough to get completely coated with sand. The result is extremely uncomfortable. It is even more uncomfortable to be the last one to make the trip, or to do a poor job of getting sandy. If that's the case, the instructor will yell at you for a while and make you do it all over again. "It pays to be a winner," the instructors say, and they are right. The effect is known as a sugar cookie.

Many of the ordeals for BUD/S students require superb teamwork skills, but few of the students have ever had to work with others with such precision. Log PT is one way to fix that deficiency because all five or six men must work in unison to get anything done with this heavy and awkward object. And the instructors demand that the logs be carried up steep sand dunes or held aloft for extended periods until the student's muscles begin to fail.

times after having come out of the cold ocean to stand in the cold wind. It is another stress, intentionally applied.

One by one people quit or are removed for injuries. Even quitting isn't easy, quick, or dignified; the trainee stands on the green painted frog footprints at one side of the "Grinder," the big blacktop space where calisthenics are performed, grasps the lanyard for the brass ship's bell attached to a column, rings the bell three times, and is gone. His green helmet liner remains in formation beside the bell with the others who've quit before him. While there is some disgrace to it, even these men get some credit (in private, away from the trainees) that it takes quite a man to get through any of BUD/S and that only a very select group even manage to get in the front door. While the quitters get credit for trying, they are, just the same, an example to those who remain.

The O Course

One of the featured entertainments is the obstacle course—the "O course" in SEAL parlance. It looks like a big sandbox with lots of play equipment: telephone poles assembled into a wide variety of structures. The BUD/S trainees are assembled here about once a week for an hour or two of play time. One after another, on command, the students dash off for a circuit of the course.

You start by running to the first event, a set of pole stumps set in the ground, their tops about two feet above the deck. You must run across them, jumping from one to the next without falling off. Then, from the last stump, leap to the top of a low wall, swing a foot over, drop to the other side, and start running. You'll go about fifty feet before you dive under a grid of barbed wire—crawl under the wire, then emerge and dash to the next structure, the net climb. A tall tower suspends a rope net that you climb to the top, swing over, and descend; the flexible net offers unstable footing and it is slow going. Once safely back on the ground, dash off to the next position, a pair of simple structures about four feet apart; you climb up on one and jump to the other, catching the crossbar across your chest; this is a favorite way to break a rib. They call this one "The Ugly Name." There are about ten more obstacles to negotiate, and your progress will be closely monitored by one of the attentive, helpful staff who are always ready with words of encouragement and advice. If you have trouble with part of the course the instructors will probably let you try the event all over again, just to make sure you get it right. Finally you return to your starting point and your time is recorded.

If you haven't done well you may get to cool off with a quick dip in the ocean, on the other side of a tall sand berm. Then, to dry off, you'll be expected to roll in the sand, then hustle back to rejoin the play group. As the trainees quickly learn, the O course is highly competitive, and people who don't do well are subject to extra, undesired attention from the instructors.

You're expected to go all out every time you run the course, and you're expected to do better every week. Minimum times for the course are published, and they get shorter every week. It is just one of the stresses that are applied to the trainees to test their motivation and physical conditioning. But, as one of the staff says, "It isn't supposed to break you, but to build up your confidence. It reveals a lot about the character of an individual. By the time you've gone through about three-fourths of it, every fiber of your muscles is burning, and you still have another quarter to go—and it's all through soft sand."

Hell Week

After five weeks of this comes the real challenge that all have heard about and dreaded: Hell Week. It starts just before midnight on the Saturday before the sixth week with a gentle wakeup call from the instructors . . . using blank M60 machine gun fire and artillery simulators as an improvised alarm clock. The noise in the compound is deafening. Besides the firing, instructors scream incessantly. Chaos reigns supreme.

The trainees begin five and a half days of virtually constant activity. They will receive an average of about twenty minutes sleep per day, if they are lucky. They will go from one event to another, constantly: running on the beach, boat drills, PT, swims. They will crawl in slime, roll in the surf, and for a little extra torture, do "log PT."

Log PT requires boat teams to lift and maneuver sections of log weighing from four hundred to six hundred pounds. If your boat team hasn't been doing well (or if the instructors think you need a little extra help with your motivation), you'll get the six-hundred-pound model. Then you can do sit-ups with it on your chest, or try holding it over your head for a while. Needless to say the whole team has to work together to do anything with it at all.

The sun comes up on the first morning, and the day proceeds much like any other at BUD/S. The sun goes down, and the trainees know that somewhere people are returning to homes and wives, to quiet evenings and friendly conversations. In the tall apartment buildings overlooking the BUD/S compound the lights will start going out around nine or ten. The PT continues. By 1:00 a.m. they are nearly all out, but the activity on the beach continues. "The only easy day was *yesterday!*" scream the instructors.

BUD/S is an unusual program in many ways, one of which is that officers and senior NCOs train alongside junior enlisted sailors. They have to perform the same exhausting evolutions required of the younger men, plus they have to lead as well. This leading petty officer directs his men as they prepare for boat drills.

The Navy calls them inflatable boat, small, or IBS, but the informal term is sometimes "itty bitty ship." Learning to use them in an effective way is another teamwork exercise and another place where it really pays to be a winner. Even when the surf is low, as it was the day these photographs were made, inexperienced students have trouble going in the right direction and occasionally get tumbled into the water when their IBS broaches.

Much of the first phase of BUD/S training concentrates on the IBD surf drills, endless launches and recoveries and races between crews. The process grinds down every student at the same time it teaches teamwork and the value of coming in first. The water is cold, the sand is abrasive, the boat is heavy, and the instructors are never happy.

When the sun comes up the next morning, the trainees will be a bit tired but will try not to think about it. All of them know what the routine is, that the really tough part is still days away. The competitions continue with boat races in the ocean and on the bay. Gradually, individuals will fail. When they do, their teams are subjected to more stress from the instructors and from the other teams.

Although they don't get any real sleep, the trainees get plenty of food. They consume about seven thousand calories a day and still lose weight.

One day melts seamlessly into another without rest. There is no alternative but to tough it out, drive through the fatigue, and keep doing what they tell you to do. It is a test of mental toughness as much as the powers of physical endurance. After four days or so people start to hallucinate. And some people start to quit. Hell Week is the most important part of the whole twenty-six-week BUD/S experience, a physical and mental challenge that is intended to put the trainees under stress that is supposed to approach that of actual combat.

The hallucinations can be rather entertaining. While enduring a long night boat race out on the ocean, after a few days with no sleep and little rest, visions begin to appear. Sometimes it is mermaids, other times people picnicking on the beach, or a strange tunnel vision.

One of the rituals is the letter home. Toward the end of the week, when everybody is off in the ozone, they are all seated before tables and provided paper and pen. "Write me a letter explaining why you want to become a SEAL!" the instructor orders. This is not an easy thing to explain after going three or four days without sleep, wallowing in the mud, doing log PT, enduring endless boat drills, and slogging through competitive events like the rubber duck races on the ocean or the sixteen-mile runs on the beach. The students tend to stare at the paper for a while before attempting to write anything. The results tend to be gibberish. Later, after Hell Week is over, these essays are returned to their authors as an amusing reminder of the tremendous stress they were under and how it affected their performance of even this simple task.

As rough as Hell Week and the whole BUD/S program is, it has been toned down considerably from the past. Trainees no longer have to wallow in the mud of the Tijuana River, essentially an open sewer, after many came down with severe (and sometimes permanent) illnesses. That ended in 1983. A somewhat healthier goo is now available right in San Diego Bay. And after one trainee died on a five-mile winter swim around San Clemente Island, the staff started taking extra precautions to deal with extreme overexertion and hypothermia. An ambulance now trails along the beach behind the trainees on the long runs through the soft sand, trailing the "goon squad," as the slower runners are called; they can quit at any time, and many do.

BUD/S has been criticized, along with other extreme selection and training programs like the army's Green Beret Q Course, for unnecessary extremes. The injuries, the high level of stress, the humiliation are all far more than anyone in civilian life or in normal military training ever must endure.

Why do it that way? As one SEAL officer explains, "One of the things I've noticed about many of the 'real world' combat operations I've been on is that you get a tremendous adrenaline rush—I call it *fear*. Once the operation begins that goes away, but on the way in you have a lot of time to sit and think. You *never* get that in a training situation! So one of the things I continually tell my troops while we are training is, 'Look, I can't give you the feeling of what it is really like to be in combat . . . because I can't shoot at you and make you hurt. It's illegal, and I wouldn't want to do that anyway. What I *can* do is to make the conditions so tough, and try to make you so tired, put you under such stress, that you will get something of a feeling of what it is like.'"

When the trainees recover from Hell Week they begin a period of study intended to prepare them for "hydrographic reconnaissance," as beach surveys are called. This involves even more time spent wallowing around in the surf, cold and miserable, while the ever-attentive staff offers suggestions and encouragement from the beach. Once through Hell Week students are treated with a bit more respect and affection by the instructors. Finally, Phase One is over.

Phase Two

Survivors of the first part of training go on to Phase Two, where they learn about diving operations. Each learns just about all there is to know about scuba, closed-circuit re-breathing systems, and dive physiology. They learn more than they ever wanted to know about the nasty things that happen to people

Opposite and overleaf: Welcome to the Grinder, a large open courtyard that serves several purposes for BUD/S instructors. It is used for daily PT where students execute seemingly endless flutter kicks, push-ups, and pull-ups. Each arrives in excellent condition, but that condition is never good enough for the instructors who demand increasing numbers of perfectly executed routines for each exercise.

Phase Three

By now the BUD/S class is beginning to see light at the end of the proverbial tunnel, and the students are pretty sure it is not from an oncoming train. They are far stronger physically and mentally than four months earlier. They've acquired a great deal of knowledge and confidence. Now they get to start putting the skills and the stamina together in practical exercises that simulate SEAL missions.

Phase Three is the demolitions/recon/land warfare part of the program. The BUD/S students learn land navigation, explosives, small unit tactics, rappelling, and patrolling skills and become expert in the employment of all the small arms and weapons used by SEALs in combat. After four weeks of classroom instruction and practical exercises, the trainees deploy to San Clemente Island for five weeks, where they put it all together.

One of the evolutions involves clearing beach obstacles like those that faced the amphibious operations of World War II—concrete blocks and steel rails dropped in shallow water to block the passage of landing craft. The students first make a careful hydrographic survey of the landing zone, noting the location of all obstacles, then plan a mission to demolish them with explosives. The quantity of explosive has to be carefully calculated, fuse measured. The students use their rubber ducks to get into the area, then dive to emplace the explosives. All the

Upper body strength is essential for many of the common tasks of SEALs and nobody even gets through the front door without the ability to do a lot of pushups and pull-ups. Those muscles are further tested and strengthened with daily PT that challenges every student's commitment and ability.

who make mistakes underwater. They learn to deal with equipment failures, lost regulators, the hazards of nitrogen narcosis. They make long swims beneath the surface and learn to navigate in the cold, murky, dark waters in which SEALs operate. After seven busy weeks the BUD/S class is missing a few more faces. The survivors have the knowledge necessary to be basic combat divers, and the program then gets really interesting.

charges are linked with det cord to ensure simultaneous explosion, and the divers are recovered to the boats. The last dive pair pulls the safety pins on the fuse-lighters, retracts the striker, and pops the igniter. Now it is time to get back to the boat. The instructors will time the delay, and it had better be within a few seconds of what was calculated. With a satisfying *whump*, the surface of the water will boil and the obstacles will (usually) be shattered.

Above and opposite: Phase III students don't escape challenging PT, even out on San Clemente Island. These men are participating in an evolution known as flight quarters that involves a short run up a hill, but with complications. Each student is required to try to imitate a navy aircraft of one sort or another while carrying a heavy, awkward object and yelling aircraft-like noises. The iron anchor chain link weighs about a hundred pounds and represents the cargo of a transport helicopter; the barrel symbolizes an aerial refueling tanker.

brutal. Although it might not be quite as dangerous as at times in the past, it is a guaranteed way to get miserable fast and stay miserable for most of six months—or more, if you get injured. And the injuries are common, almost with the intent of the staff. No other program tolerates such a high level of injuries. A lot of people outside NSW think the BUD/S program is sadistic and ought to be reformed. Commander Gary Stubblefield has an opposing view:

"It is the toughest military training in the world, and it's done that way on purpose. The army's special forces don't have anything to compare to it. It's been this way since the days of the Scouts and Raiders in World War II, a *very* difficult selection process. Most of the people who make it through the program are not premier athletes—they are *normal* people who have the ability to stick with something.

"There are injuries, some severe, in every class. But the business we are in is inherently dangerous, combat or not. If you take away the risk that goes with the training, you take away the mental stress that you put people under to know how they'll respond in the real world, in actual combat. Landing on rocks, long cold swims, surf passages—training where we have people break arms and legs—has to be part of the program. You *have* to be sure that they will stick with you when the going gets tough, and they have to know that, if you don't do things safely, there are consequences that include injury . . . or worse. Death in training is very, very rare, and it

BUD/S is probably the roughest, most demanding training and selection program in the U.S. armed forces, at least outside the covert organizations. It has been loudly criticized as excessively

happens, I think, when the student doesn't follow the rules. The deaths are an anomaly but the injuries are not—those happen when someone does something they aren't supposed to."

Jump School

But even after surviving BUD/S, a trainee is still not a fully qualified SEAL and does not wear the trident insignia of NSW. First comes three weeks at the U.S. Army's Fort Benning in Georgia, undergoing the basic airborne course. Here each will have to confront a different fear, that of jumping from an airplane, to become a fully qualified military parachutist.

The first week involves physical conditioning, and since the army school's standards are comparatively low, the BUD/S graduates manage this part of the program more or less with one hand tied behind their backs. The army instructors will try to make the experience a little bit challenging for any SEALs, rangers, marines, or others they can identify, usually requiring extra PT to keep their attention, but BUD/S graduates generally consider this part of the program a kind of vacation.

Week two teaches the basic skills of military parachuting: donning the parachute, actions inside the aircraft, door position, jump-master commands, proper exit techniques, emergency procedures, and the parachute landing fall (PLF). The students endlessly practice door position, exits, and PLFs from training aids: the suspended harness, the thirty-four-foot tower, the C-130 mock-up.

Finally, they start week three, Jump Week. Five jumps are required, three "Hollywood" daylight jumps without combat equipment plus one night jump and one jump with a loaded rucksack and weapons container. The night jump is usually a sunrise or sunset jump rather than one in full darkness.

Jump school is actually a lot of fun for many of the people who attend, and the BUD/S graduates hardly work up a sweat.

The jumps are often exciting, the instructors fairly civilized, the drop zone a soft, fluffy plowed field. The last jump is generally done on Friday morning, and students often invite friends and relatives to watch from nearby bleachers. Then the army instructors break out the silver wings of a qualified military parachutist and pin them to the shirts of the students.

Martial arts and unarmed combat skills are taught early and often at BUD/S. *Hans Halberstadt/www.militaryphoto.com Opposite:* The O course is run many times by BUD/S students and each must show a better time on every session than the previous session.

Phase II students spend many hours in the pool where the water is clearer than the ocean but not much warmer. Before learning any of the skills of a combat swimmer or diver, each must learn to be comfortable and safe in the water, even with his hands tied behind him.

64

The Budweiser

Completion of the basic airborne course is the final academic portion of the program required to join a SEAL delivery vehicle (SDV) team, but the students are still not bona fide SEALs. First, each man is assigned to a team where he must complete a six-month probationary period. It is still possible to fail, and individuals occasionally are filtered out, even now, if they don't fit into the team or fail to meet spec somehow. But at the end of the six months, a year or more after starting the process, a few young men will pin on the big, gold symbol of NSW and finally be able to call themselves SEALs.

They enter a tiny, select community with a big reputation that sometimes gets in the way of business. Within the military SEALs are sometimes known as "cowboys" or "glass-eaters" who glory in their superman image. Instead they find a different kind of man on the teams: extremely confident without bravado, a man with tremendous talents and abilities, a person who knows his own limit. "We like to think of ourselves as quiet professionals," one says.

Rear Admiral Ray Smith says: "We are essentially a *people* business. We use a lot of exotic equipment—scuba, parachutes, radios—but all those things are peripheral to the essence of what we are. Our focus at BUD/S is on the human being, the nature of the person we want to have come on a SEAL team and do the things we have to do—always has been, always will. The finest equipment in the world (which we have) is not sufficient to accomplish our missions. You'll see guys in BUD/S who don't look very impressive physically—little guys, young guys—who'll surprise you and make it through. You can *never* successfully predict who will make it through! You can't measure what is inside the individual without subjecting him to BUD/S. In fact, this is a course in the development of human potential; all we are trying to do is to make the young man understand that the limits of the human being are practically unlimited."

Of the fifty or sixty students who begin BUD/S, the staff will tell you there will be five or six who *know* they are going to complete the program, no matter what, and that there is no stopping them. There are another five or six who don't really want to be here, are not really ready for the challenge, and who will never be SEALs. In the middle are the 80 percent the

Escape from the trials and tribulations of BUD/S is never far away. All it takes is three strokes on the bell, and the student is immediately removed from the program and sent back to wherever he came from.

instructors focus their efforts on. They probe for the fears that every man has—a fear of heights, of water, of jumping from high platforms—and each is confronted daily with his perceived limitations and pushed past them. "You can't call 'time out' in combat," one of the instructors says, "and that's what we try to teach them here."

Officers and enlisted personnel go through training together, unlike some other programs where officers sometimes get an easier ride. Both suffer and perform equally at BUD/S. It is a team-building system, developing trust up and down the chain of command. About 35 new officers and 250 enlisted personnel graduate from BUD/S annually and join the world of SPECWARCOM on the SEAL, special boat, and SDV teams.

Chapter 4

MOVEMENT TO CONTACT

SEALs and most other operators in American special units are generally HALO trained; the acronym stands for high-altitude (aircraft exit), low-opening (parachute deployment). HALO jumps involve exiting from aircraft at altitudes between about ten and thirty-five thousand feet above ground level; at such heights the sound of an aircraft is inaudible to a person on the ground. And since such jumps are always made at night, the whole process is essentially undetectable. The jumper's parachute is deployed only a thousand feet or so above the ground and he then unhooks his rucksack from the harness, uses his toes to hold it while he steers toward a suitable landing site, then drops the ruck to the end of its lowering line just before landing. Successful graduates of the HALO school are authorized to wear one of the more unusual military qualification badges.

Despite the way it is shown in the movies, the business of going into combat is a lot more complicated than picking up your weapon and following some resolute-looking lieutenant or sergeant who growls, "Okay, men, follow me!" The movies always manage to leave out all the paperwork, meetings, and related homework that comes first. In fact, it is just about impossible for American combat units to go off to battle without a great deal of this stuff. It can take weeks to prepare an operation of any kind, conventional or covert, but at the end of this long process will finally come two quite interesting management/staff meetings. The first of these is called a Warning Order; the other is called the Patrol Leader's Order.

The Warning Order

Before SEALs and SBS crews go anywhere or do anything, the mission has to be authorized, approved, and planned. A long time ago the units did most of this internally, but for the last decade or so, the missions have been conceived and tasked from outside NAVSPECWARCOM. Somewhere during the process somebody decides it is okay to actually let the teams know that they can cancel those weekend plans. The way this is done is that the selected team is herded into a compartment or room, the area is secured, the doors are closed, and somebody, normally the unit commander, will issue a warning order.

In various forms, warning orders have been around since the Mongol hordes, since Attila, since Alexander the Great. In its short form it sounds something like, "We're going to break camp in the morning before sunrise and attack the infidels, sack their town, and put the place to the torch. Bring your sword, spear, and all your armor. Questions?"

The modern version is more complicated, but the idea is identical. It gives the people involved an idea, usually incomplete, of what they are going to be doing and what they should do to prepare. The formal version (used by the army and marines as well) includes a brief description of the situation; the mission; general instructions, including organization, uniform, weapons, chain of command, schedule, including time for the more detailed patrol order, and for inspections and rehearsals; and specific instructions for subordinate leaders and individuals.

Everybody then scurries around, collecting weapons, demolition material, MREs, fresh batteries for the radios, and night vision goggles. *Nobody* gets to call home and say, "Guess what, Honey, I'm not gonna be home on time tonight 'cause we're off to defend freedom and democracy. . . ."

Instead, they just don't come home in the evening. Sooner or later the families might get some extremely vague information, but that's one of the costs of admission to the special operations and rapid-deployment military communities. And not only do these call-ups happen for real world events, they are called for training, too, with irregular frequency.

The idea behind the warning order is that once the order comes down to the unit, a fixed amount of time will be specified before the operation is supposed to be executed—perhaps

One of the basic missions of SEAL teams is vessel board, search, and seizure (VBSS). Getting aboard the vessel is only the first part of the problem and that is being done here by climbing up a skinny little ladder, and it is less fun than you might think, especially when you are loaded down with weapons and gear, out in the middle of the ocean, on a black night with a heavy sea running. Then you swing back and forth, crashing against the hull as the vessel rolls. If you're lucky, the crew won't notice they have visitors till your team enters the wheelhouse and takes control of the ship. *Eric Logsdon, U.S. Navy SPECWARCOM*

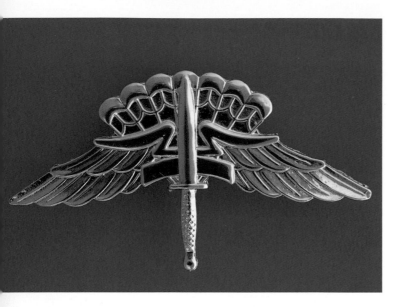

Very few members of the military wear the HALO School qualification badge on their dress uniforms but the technique of jumping from an aircraft at extreme high altitude is another covert insertion technique used by SEALs. The course is taught by the U.S. Army and is attended by members of all the U.S. Special Operations Forces.

twelve hours. The platoon or squad leader is expected to take a third of that time to make his own preliminary plan, and allocate two-thirds of the time to the subordinates to do their preparation and rehearsals. While it often doesn't work out that neatly, the idea is a sound one and is applied as much as circumstances permit.

SOPs

Each platoon has its own set of standard operating procedures (SOPs), its own identity, its unique reputation and subculture, all based somewhat on the characters on the team.

SOPs make planning and executing operations far faster and more efficient than otherwise. When a patrol leader's order is issued, only the unique details of the mission need to be discussed—radio frequencies, rendezvous points, routes in and out of the objective, commander's intent. All the other essentials—patrol order of march, actions on contact, reaction to ambush, individual responsibilities—all these things have been long since memorized as a kind of "company policy" that doesn't need repeating. Most of the members of the teams, like Bob Gormly's SEAL Team Two, had known each other for four or five years and could just about execute an operation without a word ever being spoken.

Patrol Leader's Order

The five-paragraph format used to formally brief the mission has been in use since World War I, its format memorized by millions of servicemen over the years. It forces the unit to plan logically to deal with an extremely stressful and dangerous experience. The elements of the order are the situation, the mission, the details of the execution, how the mission will be supported and supplied, and command and communications. Depending on the complexity of the mission, the orders brief can last a few minutes or six hours; an hour or so is typical. SEALs may get some of the most difficult and dangerous missions, but they also get some of the very best and most expensive intelligence support, often custom-made for the specific mission. This will

Here and overleaf Special purpose insertion/extraction (SPIE) rigging is seldom used tactically now, but once was a very important way of recovering operators from the jungles of Southeast Asia.

almost always include overhead imagery, photographs from all altitudes, from low level all the way up to the secret satellites like the KA-11. There may be radio and telephone intercepts, and reports from agents in the operations area. And (in extreme and rare cases) a prisoner may be snatched out of the target area, brought back to chat with the team, and held until the mission concludes and the team is safely extracted.

SEALs like to rehearse their missions, and if it is practical to do so, some kind of run-through will be done. This might be no more than a detailed brainstorming conference somewhere in the bowels of a submarine, or it might involve the construction of a mock-up of a target and a complete rehearsal of the entire mission ashore. Regardless, once the patrol leader's order has

It is called helo-cast and recovery, and is another fundamental way to deliver and retrieve SEALs. When they are inserted, the helicopter flies about fifteen feet above the water while maintaining a very slow forward motion; the SEALs drop feet first, close together without the danger of one landing on another. Recovery is done from about the same altitude. The crew drops a ladder and the SEALs clamber back aboard through the rotorwash and ocean spray.

been given, none of the players will be going anywhere or doing anything except preparing to launch into the op area.

When it is time to go to work, SEALs commute in dramatic and dangerous ways. Although trained for insertion to an operating area by parachute, that's really not the SEALs' forte. Except in rare instances, the mission will begin with an insertion over or under the surface of the water.

At any time there are SEALs deployed aboard U.S. submarines operating around the world, waiting for world events to call for their services. When the orders trickle down the chain of command, the SEALs plan their mission and use the most stealthy technique of all to drop in on the enemy—submarine insertion.

U.S. subs have a small chamber, the "escape trunk," installed forward of the sail. This little chamber has two functions, the

The light strike vehicle or desert patrol vehicle (DPV) is a modified version of a civilian dune buggy that saw extensive use during the first Gulf War but that has been largely replaced by modified HMMWV "Humvees" in recent years. SEAL Team Three is reported to still be using them because of their blazing speed on open desert terrain. DPVs have been equipped with Mk 19s, M2 machine guns, AT4 rocket launchers, and even a low-recoil cannon.

first allowing for trapped submariners to escape a boat sunken in shallow water, and the second (a secondary use) allowing for the deployment and recovery of combat swimmers.

Locking out of a sub is not for the faint of heart. The swimmers don their wet suits and their combat equipment, collect weapons, explosives, and related equipment, and prepare to enter the chamber; scuba or Draeger rigs are, believe it or not, optional. Then, one after another, they climb into the chamber, a spherical space about six feet across. Up to five combat swimmers can crowd into the chamber, but all will be extremely cramped and uncomfortable. Even among trained and experienced SEALs panic sometimes occurs as the water is slowly allowed in. There are mouthpieces and air lines installed in the chamber, and it is possible to use the sub's own air supply for breathing until the chamber is unlocked and it is time to leave. But SEALs normally use their own rigs—if they have any. It is quite possible to ascend to the surface without scuba or re-breather, and SEALs train for

this free ascent or blow-and-go technique, as well as the reverse technique required to come back aboard.

The sub will slither in as close to shore as the skipper and the SEALs can agree on. Subs are not normally content to be in shallow water close to a hostile coast; SEALs are normally not pleased to swim in from over the horizon. So the typical mission will bring the SSN attack sub into a mile or two off the coast on a dark and hopefully stormy night. The sub will come up to a depth of about forty feet, bring the periscope up for a quick peek at the neighborhood, then bring it back down. The 'scope makes a fair radar reflector, and if somebody is working a surface search radar tweaked for such targets, there could be a problem. So the sub crew gets extremely edgy about this kind of mission.

A typical insertion out of the chamber will have one man go out first, with scuba, and rig the Zodiac stored in the sail locker on deck. The boat will have to be taken to the surface while a tether is left attached to the submarine. This entire complex

Above and opposite: Fast roping is a very common insertion technique that can deliver a SEAL squad onto a beach, oil platform, or ship's deck within seconds. The helicopter crew swoops in to position about thirty feet above the deck and comes to a hover over a suitable landing zone. Each SEAL wears heavy leather gloves and, on the command of the helicopter crew chief, grasps the two-inch rope, then swings out and begins his controlled decent, keeping about ten feet between himself and the man below him on the rope. The technique requires excellent upper body strength to execute safely.

activity is done in darkness, almost entirely by touch, and takes about half an hour. When the diver has the boat properly infiltrated and on a tow, he signals the sub to send up the rest of the SEALs. Even this isn't quick or easy: he can flash a light signal at the periscope if the sub skipper is willing to raise it, he can swim down and rap on the hull, or he can even go back in the lockout chamber, repressurize and have a chat via microphone.

Usually, though, a simple rap on the hull will do it. Then the next batch of divers cram into the chamber, the water level rises, and finally somebody has to wriggle a hand over to the valves and latches that will open the hatch.

"You get into there, you've got all this weight on you, you close the bottom hatch, you stand there, doubled over—tanks on your back, equipment in your arms—three to five people jammed in there. Then somebody has to find a way to reach over to the valve so you can start to flood the chamber. There are some guys who are just more nervous about all this—everybody jammed in that small space, water coming up to your neck. I've seen guys panic in there."

It takes a long time, usually in cold, high seas, for the seven or eight men to rig the boats and exit the sub for a typical mission of this type. Hypothermia and seasickness will be a problem for those already in the boat up on the surface while the nervousness of the sub crew will be a problem for those still aboard. Even the rubber boats have a radar return signature, and if anybody is looking, the whole operation can suddenly become a target instead of a weapon. It is a very nervous time. But then, after perhaps a couple of hours, you're all set and it's time to go ashore.

Dry Deck Shelter

There is an easier way, a bolt-on chamber that is called the dry deck shelter (DDS). While it operates on the same principle as the lock-out chamber, it is far larger. The DDS is big enough to accommodate a whole platoon, with dive gear and rubber boats, radios and demolitions. It will also accommodate the SDV, the SEAL-scooter that is designed for zipping around underwater. Besides these handy features, it converts to a hyperbaric chamber for treating a diver who's been "bent" from staying under too long, too deep, and acquires the painful, potentially fatal condition called decompression sickness.

While the general insertion technique for the DDS is the same as with the lock-out chamber, it is a lot faster and a lot less

Daylight parachute insertions with the old MC1-1B parachute are not a common event except in training. This parachute is one of the first widely used canopies that can easily be steered but has been largely replaced by the MC-4 ram-air type among most special operations units.

crowded. The whole evolution goes faster, much to the delight of the submarine crew.

To the Beach

Once everybody's safely in a Zodiac, the SEALs time to break out the paddles or fire up the engine and head to the beach. Several hundred meters offshore, well outside the surf zone, a pair of divers—the scout swimmers—slip over the gunwales of the Zodiac and, with weapons at the ready, move in to secure the section of beach where the landing is intended. After a quick check of the area, they signal the boats to come in. The rubber ducks run in through the surf, everybody alert for enemy contact, and the boats are promptly pulled up across the high water mark and either hidden or buried.

Once secure on the beach, the SEALs are ready to execute the mission. If it is a patrol or a direct action strike deep inland,

the squad (or perhaps platoon if two boats have come ashore) assembles itself and prepares to move off into the hinterland without a word being spoken. Communication is done with hand and arm signals, visible and instantly recognizable even on dark, cloudy nights.

Out front, leading the patrol, is the point man who navigates the patrol to the objective. This is traditionally the most dangerous, difficult position in the patrol order, requiring superb land navigation skills and an extremely high level of alertness to the possibility of contact with enemy forces. A point man can walk you right into the kill zone of an ambush, or halt the patrol safely outside. Such choices can be (and often have been) the difference of life and death for an entire patrol. When contact with the enemy is made, the man on point is typically the first to fire or the first to die.

The point man's preferred weapon in wooded terrain is often not a rifle or machine gun but a military version of a standard 12-gauge shotgun, loaded with five rounds of "double-shot" (size 00) buckshot. These are large, bullet-sized lead pellets that spread out in a lethal cone of destruction. One pellet will kill out to a range of about a hundred meters, sometimes farther; at closer ranges, particularly within about ten meters, a well-placed load will punch a gaping hole through a torso, or rip off an arm or a head. It is the approximate equivalent of firing seven or so bullets at exactly the same instant in the same general direction.

An alternative load is the flachette round, with tiny steel darts in place of the buckshot. While these are not nearly as lethal or destructive individually, there are many more of them, and they produce a denser cloud of projectiles, a handy way of providing a group of enemy soldiers at close range with something to think about besides the SEAL patrol. They are lethal out to several hundred meters.

There's yet another handy 12-gauge round for the point man's shotgun, a single, heavy slug useful for opening locked doors and disabling machinery or electronics in one quick, brutal way. It is accurate out to a range of about five feet, maybe six. If it hits something, the target stays hit. This is no precision munition, but it will punch a hole in the cast-iron block of an automobile engine, or the concrete wall of a house or bunker—or, if they cooperate, a whole row of enemy soldiers.

Riflemen

If the point man bumps into a bad guy at close range and gets the first shot off effectively, the patrol has the choice of either "going to ground" and duking it out with the opposing team or making a run for the beach. In either case the point man's shotgun will soon have limited utility—it will be out of range, out of ammunition, or both. That's why there are several riflemen on a normal patrol, each with an M16 rifle and five or six thirty-round magazines stashed in their load-carrying web gear.

M16A2 and CAR15

The M16A2 rifle is almost the same weapon that the fathers of some of today's SEALs carried and fought with in Vietnam a generation ago. It's no longer the most exotic weapon on the battlefield, or on the teams, but it is still a good, light, accurate, effective weapon that has proven itself in countless battles. The latest version is more reliable than the first, which had a failure-to-feed problem for a while. The A2 also lacks the "full-auto" feature of the original, a modification based on the discovery that in the heat of combat the weapon was being used as a "bullet hose," ineffectively spraying rounds downrange. Instead, the rifle has a BURST position on the selector switch on the left side of the receiver, above the trigger; this permits three-round bursts that economize on ammunition while encouraging the rifleman to aim rather than point the weapon.

While the basic rifle issued to SEALs is essentially the same as the M16A2 issued to U.S. Army and Marine Corps infantry privates (and just about everybody else too), the SEALs' version tends to be an upgraded, customized weapon with specialized sights and a collapsible stock or a compact version of the M16 that has been popular with special operators for the last twenty years, the CAR15. This little squirt gun uses essentially the same receiver components as the bigger M16, but with an ingenious collapsible stock assembly and shorter barrel. It trades bulk for a little fragility and a slightly greater inclination to jam. The decision to carry the CAR15 or M16 is—as with similar decisions on a team—partly a matter of personal choice. SEALs, along with other special operators, are permitted to exercise a lot more latitude in the choice of accessories than are troopers in more conventional units.

Depending on the particular mission, the sights installed may be a night-vision scope or a laser aim-point system. The night-vision scope amplifies existing light and presents the shooter with a magnified, green and black picture of the target through a somewhat conventional rifle scope. The other device mounts a small laser pointer under the barrel; once activated it puts a bright red dot where the bullet will strike. You don't need to peep through a scope or iron sights—just put the red dot on your intended victim and squeeze. It is not a long-range, sniping

system; but for night combat in confined spaces it is often the system of choice.

The M16 fires a small, 5.56mm (.223-caliber) bullet at high velocity. This makes for a very flat trajectory and a lot of retained energy at practical ranges. The Vietnam-era version of the M16 was supposed to be good out to about 300 meters; today's weapon/cartridge combination is rated to 460 meters—about a quarter of a mile. That means that a trained rifleman can hit a man-sized target at that range with about 50 percent of his carefully aimed shots. The bullet, of course, is lethal out to a couple of miles, but hitting things with it at extreme ranges has more to do with luck than gun control.

MP4 and MP5

The M16 and CAR15 are not the only choices for a SEAL rifleman to take on a mission. His weapon can be almost anything that he and the patrol leader think is appropriate. One favorite alternative is the Heckler & Koch (H&K) MP5 "room broom" submachine gun. It fires the diminutive 9mm Parabellum pistol round and is well matched to the laser aim-point sight system for urban combat situations. It is extremely compact—you can wear it under a jacket for those formal events. Like the shotgun, it is accurate and effective only out to fifty meters or so, and its projectiles aren't guaranteed to have the desired effect. But you can carry (and shoot) a lot of those little 9mm rounds; if you squirt a burst of them into a bunker, those inside will probably wish you hadn't.

The bigger brother of the MP5 is a beefy submachine gun called the MP4, brought to you by those fine folks at H&K, builders of fine military weapons used around the world. Both of these German weapons possess a quality that, in many ways, is more important than accuracy, hitting power, weight, or rate of fire: when you pull the trigger the gun goes *bang*. This reputation for reliability has sold a lot of H&K weapons to a lot of operators, and it is the reason you'll so often see them, dripping sea water and covered with sand, coming across a beach in the hands of SEALs.

Silencers

On the muzzles of all these rifles and submachine guns you'll sometimes see tubular devices about eight inches long and an inch and a half in diameter. These are sound suppressers, or silencers as they are sometimes called. For weapons such as the 9mm H&Ks, with subsonic ammunition, they can convert the loud report to a subtle pop by slowing the propellant gasses as

On the occasions when SEALs can be delivered to a beach in more or less dry condition, the squad or element sets up a security perimeter before moving off toward the hinterland. Since SEALs are few in number and have relatively few guns in any fight, they are extremely careful about when, where, and who they intentionally engage.

The caving ladder is a simple tool used by recreational cave explorers. Constructed of thin cable and lightweight aluminum rungs, it rolls into a compact bundle. SEALs find them handy for boarding all sorts of targets whose residents might not want visitors. These swimmers are practicing the techniques required to take down an oil platform, a mission that uses many of the muscles and teamwork skills acquired at BUD/S.

they rush out the muzzle behind the bullet. This can be a very handy feature in those sneaky, close-in fights that SEALs sometimes encounter.

Suppressers work on the M16, too, but not nearly as well. The standard ammunition for the weapon is designed to produce very high velocities, far faster than the speed of sound. Much of the noise from the firing of an M16 comes from the sonic boom produced by the bullet's flight through air. Even so, some of the noise can be reduced, and suppressers are often attached even to M16s, particularly in urban combat situations. As with the aim-point and night sights and so many other tools of the trade, suppressers have their specialized role in the SEALs' bag of tricks.

M203 Grenade Launcher

One of the most interesting and useful weapons you'll find carried on a SEAL mission is the M203 grenade launcher, a fairly simple weapon with a complex variety of ammunition and uses. It isn't much more than a short length of aluminum tube with a breech block and trigger assembly. It bolts to an M16 rifle, under the barrel; the magazine provides the hand grip. The 203 fires a 40mm cartridge with one of several warheads. It is a bit like a mortar, although it is called a grenade launcher. Its lobbing trajectory allows you to toss projectiles over berms and other forms of cover that your opponent may use to hide from direct fire weapons. Within about two or three hundred meters you should, with training, be able to put one of

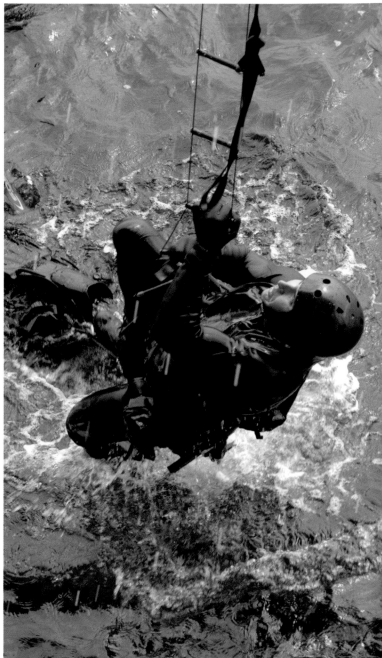

the rounds through a doorway or bunker aperture (although it might take a few tries).

Projectiles come in several flavors. There is a high explosive model that is one of the most popular. It will reach out about five hundred meters and will kill or injure anybody within about five meters of impact, a useful device when enemy infantry are closing in on your position. The M203 will also fire illumination rounds, like the mortar, that will light up the battlefield at night, along with tear gas, white phosphorus, and flachette rounds for other times and places.

M60 Machine Gun

A SEAL squad with an inland patrol mission will carry plenty of "organic" firepower in the form of two stripped down M60 machine guns. The M60 is another old design that has been improved since the years when the dad of today's SEAL carried one back in the "big war." It fires the bigger 7.62mm (.308-caliber) NATO cartridge, delivering accurate, high-volume fire on area targets at ranges well beyond what the M16 can effectively engage.

It is a heavy weapon, with heavy ammunition, often cursed on those long walks in the woods and swamps—until, that is, the opposing team materializes out of the woodwork, spoiling for a fight. Then the M60 is worth its weight in gold or blood.

If this seems like a lot of choices, it is. A team commander explains his personal attitude toward weapons used by SEALs:

"I think we really do need a variety of weapons on the teams. Certain operations call for specific capabilities. I also don't think every guy should have a different weapon, just because he has his own personal preference. I should be able to switch magazines with the guy next to me if I run out and he hasn't. But, for the rifleman, the choice can be between the M14, the MP5, or the M16. The MP5 is for use in brush or urban combat situations. The M16 is a good, general, all-around weapon, and you can put the M203 under it. The M14 has extra power for penetration and range.

"Riflemen are for engaging *point* targets and they should be shooting single shots; personally, I don't even believe in three-round bursts. I don't even believe in double-tap [firing two quick shots at a target instead of one], although the idea is currently quite popular. If you put the first shot where you're supposed to, you don't *need* another one! If you need another one, pull the trigger again. Why waste ammunition? You should be calm enough under fire to know what you are doing rather than just opening up full-auto and spraying the riverbank.

"The automatic weapon man is not to take out point targets; he's supposed to keep the enemy's head down and to give you covering fire while the riflemen take care of the point targets."

Above, right, and opposite: Combat swimmers set up a defensive security perimeter as they come ashore, listening for approaching vehicles and watching for beach patrols. The insertion process begins well off shore; the swimmers come to the surface just beyond the surf zone, and then spend long minutes observing the beach and hinterland for any sort of activity. They are essentially invisible here—unless they are expected and a sentry is waiting for their arrival. When it seems safe to proceed, each man slips the heel straps of his fins over his arm where they are out of the way but easily accessible if a hasty exit is required. Once across the beach, the fins will be secured on the swimmer's back using a snap-link.

Combat swimmers always operate in pairs for mutual safety and security. These SEALs are equipped almost exactly as those on the early teams with the exception that they are wearing woodland-pattern BDUs over their wet suits. Both are equipped with the same H&K MP-5 submachinegun that has been so popular with special operations forces for many years.

RTO

The patrol can be far from a friendly face but still be in contact with the civilized world, thanks to the battery-powered high technology that the RTO (an old expression, short for radio telephone operator) carries. There are any number of systems he can carry, and with some of them you can chat with the big bosses in Washington and in the Pentagon—although that's not usually something the team will think is a good idea.

That's because you're on the ground, with eyes on the target, and the admirals and the assistant secretary of defense sitting next to him are both in a comfortable room in a safe place. When the sun goes down, they will go off for cocktails somewhere, have a nice dinner, and watch TV. You will crawl through the mud and perhaps have people shoot at you, all while attempting to do the bidding of these "experts" with the clean fingernails, thanks to that little "satcom" transceiver carried by the RTO.

Satellite radios are now extremely compact and can easily be taken along on operations with a very moderate weight penalty. They allow the team leader to communicate with almost anybody, almost anywhere (if he can get a channel on the satellite). That, believe it or not, can be a real problem. Although you can call for help from almost anywhere on the globe with these little systems, if some politician in the "puzzle palace" comes up with a wild hair idea, they can call *you* and task you with this death-defying scheme, all from the comfort and safety of Washington, D.C.

The RTO is, in some ways, a pack mule for the patrol leader; he carries the radio and operates it, but under the control of the patrol leader, whom the RTO shadows. The RTO is, along with

the officer, a natural target for any sensible sniper on the opposing team who manages to identify and engage the patrol. The radio is the patrol's link to the close air support gunships overhead, the naval gunfire support offshore, and the slicks (unarmed helicopters) ready to swoop in to rescue the patrol in an emergency. By eliminating the RTO and his equipment, the enemy can isolate the squad and chop it to small pieces. That's why RTOs fold the aerials of their radios down and do their best to look as innocent as possible.

A funny thing about these radios, though, is that—despite their usually excellent reliability and reception—at moments like these they may suddenly stop working. As one officer explains:

"We have better communications now than we used to, but that works both ways. If I need to get ahold of somebody I probably can. It also means that guy can get ahold of me—and give me directions that I might not want. I can remember two times, during 1965 operations in Vietnam, when somebody tried to tell me what to do while I was on the ground. I didn't like it—and in one case I turned off the radio. Now, if the National Command Authority wants to talk to me while I'm on a hot operation, they very well may. This is not necessarily a good thing. To me, the guy on the scene calls the shots. He should receive *nothing* from those guys except support, when he calls up and asks for it. We make a plan and should stick to the plan, unless the guy on the ground wants to do differently. Now, if somebody has some information that can help you, if they see a platoon of enemy, for example, coming down the road toward you, they ought to be able to let you know. But don't tell me to go left or right in reaction to that platoon—let *me* make that decision!

"We have a tendency, because we have such good communications, to let responsibility slip upward where sometimes it doesn't belong. Look what happened at Desert One [the failed Iranian hostage rescue mission]. Jimmy Carter was in the position where he could call up Colonel Beckwith [the on-scene commander] and tell him what to do. I don't like that! Most people in the SEALs don't like that. Some people submit to that. And some people automatically get their hackles up—don't submit to it; put the radio down and say 'Dang, something just went wrong with the radio!' The problem with letting decisions be made someplace, with letting somebody else be responsible, is that I'm still responsible for the people who are with me. I want to make the decision for what happens once we launch the mission. Tell me what to do *before* I leave, and then if I buy off on it, fine. Just don't tell me what to do once I'm out there. While we have the advantage of better communications, we get with that the disadvantage of potential micro-management by people not on the scene."

Patrol Leader

The patrol leader on a SEAL operation is going to be one of the platoon's two commissioned officers, the platoon leader (normally a lieutenant) or executive officer (lieutenant junior grade or possibly ensign). The role of a combat leader is an odd kind of combination of duties that sometimes conflict. A combat leader has two heavy responsibilities: to complete the mission and to preserve the force. That means that the leader takes himself and his followers to complete a mission that, in war, will probably involve great hazard. How much hazard is sometimes influenced by the officer; it may depend on how much risk he's willing to take in a given time and place. Just how important the mission is he has to judge. He has to judge how much it is worth, in time, effort, ammunition, and the blood of his men. So the patrol leader is stuck in the middle, with a responsibility upward, to his commanders who've tasked him with a mission, and downward, to his followers who trust his judgment.

The officer is part of the platoon, and he is aloof from it. He guards his men, is responsible for their welfare as a parent is for a child—and may send them knowingly to their deaths or dismemberment. He is trained, at Annapolis or Officer Candidate School (OCS), to be careful to avoid playing favorites and developing the natural kind of friendships that are common among civilians—fraternization, it is called.

The officer discovers, early in his career, that while the troops will automatically salute and call him *sir*, the respect may not be sincere. An officer learns that respect is earned in two phases: first through the commissioning process that awards gold bars and officer rank, then all over again in the units where real competence and leadership are demonstrated. For SEALs there is another part, BUD/S, where officers must perform alongside the enlisted sailors, suffer all the same insults and indignities, the same stresses and fatigue. It is an important part of the bonding between the leaders and the followers in the SEALs.

As officer candidates quickly learn at Annapolis, NROTC, or OCS, it's a complicated business to lead men in combat. It is a bit like leading an orchestra; you don't need to be the best player of every instrument, but you have to know perfectly what each can do—then to be able to make sure its resources are integrated into the big score. But the terrible, wonderful thing about military operations is that they are, always and invariably, partially improvisations. There is an old military saying: No plan survives contact with the enemy. That means that no matter how well you think you've prepared, something is going to go wrong. And when it does, one person needs to be responsible for selecting an alternative course of action. That's what officers are for.

The platoon leader will normally have been personally given the mission and then designed the plan, with help from above

Combat swimmers employ a variety of weapons but the Heckler & Koch MP5 9mm submachine gun has been a favorite among SEALs in close-quarters combat for many years. The MP5 has several excellent virtues as a weapon: it is reliable and not likely to jam, it is controllable and easy to keep on target, and it easily mounts a very effective sound suppressor that reduces the sound signature to a quiet pop.

and below. He takes the plan to the field and makes it happen with the help of his SEALs. When the shooting starts he is expected to direct, manage, and control the firing. When the ambush is triggered, he initiates it with a squeeze of the trigger, or the clacker for the Claymore. His M16 magazines may be full of nothing but tracers, which he uses to indicate targets for the rest of the squad to fire on.

On the march, the patrol leader will typically be toward the front of the line. He may take the point sometimes, but usually will be the number two man, where he can provide direction for the man on point and still control the squad in case of contact. The RTO will be right behind the patrol leader, however, wherever he is.

Tail Gunner

The two most vulnerable areas for the patrol are its front and its back; it will either bump into trouble, or trouble will come sneaking up on it. That's why both the man on point and the last man in line, the tail gunner, have to be especially sharp. The tail gunner will probably have one of the squad's cut-down M60 machine guns—and eyes in the back of his head.

In actual combat, on deep penetration missions, he'll probably carry a variety of goodies to help break contact if the patrol finds itself compromised and on the run. Then he'll pull out the tear gas grenades, the devastating WP (white phosphorous) grenades, and perhaps a Claymore to rig as a booby trap against the pursuers.

Chapter 5

ACTIONS AT THE OBJECTIVE

Under the dubious glow of an illumination round from an M203 grenade launcher, a SEAL squad assaults an objective during a night training exercise in the desert. Even with NODs (night observation devices), SEALs have to be extremely careful about the conduct of small unit operations because of the danger of "friendly fire" incidents. Training for SEAL missions is sometimes as dangerous as operations on the "two-way rifle range." *Eric Logsdon, U.S. Navy SPECWARCOM*

As mentioned before, SEALs have five different general types of missions to perform: direct action, recon, foreign internal defense, unconventional warfare, and counterterrorist. This is a broad spectrum of responsibilities for a small organization, no matter how well trained or funded. Some of these are primary SEAL missions; others are secondary.

Counterterrorist operations, for example, are really the stock-in-trade for Delta, the army's superb, extremely exclusive counterterrorist unit. The men (and—promise not to tell where you heard this—women) in Delta are going to get the call for such operations except under extreme circumstances. SEALs are trained and prepared to execute the operation, and there are a few "long hair" team members available for extremely covert ops, but it is hardly a prime talent for aquatic warriors.

Likewise, foreign internal defense (FID) and unconventional warfare (UW) are prime army missions that are backed up by SEALs. Both require the language skills and charm of a diplomat, the charisma of an evangelist, and the patience of a saint. The FID mission turns out to be one that a few SEALs excel at, about five guys of the two hundred or so on a team, according to one team commander. This mission occupies a few SEALs in Latin America now, and it kept a lot busy during the workup to Desert Storm in training Saudi and other Arab naval personnel in the Gulf. As one of the team commanders says:

"I think we're quite good at the traditional Green Beret mission of foreign internal defense; we have a very high degree of success when we include foreign military personnel in our operations. For some reason we've thrown that back to the army. We were very good in the Gulf when we took two or three SEALs and used them with ten or twelve host-nation personnel. We 'force-multiplied.' We had all the advantages of the host-nation expertise, plus our skills and experience in executing that type of operation. It was a Cracker Jack setup!"

But it is not one most SEALs find very appealing. It takes many months of study at the Defense Language Institute (DLI) at Monterey, California, to acquire the skill to speak Arabic, for example, or Estonian, and that means time away from the teams. Unconventional warfare is the behind-the-lines version of FID, and hasn't really been used much since World War II—although it is still sitting there as a tasking for the special operations forces.

A pair of SEALs head for a special operations craft-riverine (SOC-R) standing by to assist with the exfiltration honors. The SOC-R is a fairly new addition to the fleet of boats available to support SEAL missions. It is very fast, heavily armed, and can accommodate a full squad and all their gear, weapons, and prisoners. Once everybody's aboard, the guys from the SBSs will spin the boat around, roar down the river at up to forty-three knots, and light up any targets on the shore that offer a threat. *Eric Logsdon, U.S. Navy SPECWARCOM*

So the principal missions, the ones that get the attention, the time, the rehearsals, are recon and strike. The first is stealthy and the second isn't.

Recons, Deep and Shallow

Despite all the wonderful, expensive technology that has gone into intelligence gathering, with billions of dollars spent on camera systems for aircraft and satellites, there is still no substitute for having someone go ashore for a hands-on, eyes-on study of a potential target. One of the lessons learned from Urgent Fury was that overhead intel only begins to provide essential planning information and that things like landing zones can look completely different to a helicopter pilot than to a high-flying aircraft—with potentially catastrophic results.

Although not as glamorous as the strike missions, recon ops are just as important now as ever. SEALs still get tasked with these jobs, and it is their particular art form.

The recon mission can be just about anything, anywhere. The classic one, of course, is the beach recon preceding an amphibious operation. While the Marines think their own recon guys can do this better than anybody, SEALs politely disagree. While it doesn't get much attention, it is still a tremendously important mission when you consider how much investment the United States has in putting marines across the beach anywhere in the world. The memory of Tarawa half a century ago haunts the marines—and the navy too. Beach recons, consequently, are a big part of the course of instruction at BUD/S, where they're called hydrographic surveys. They can be as simple or as detailed as you and your commanders want—and as circumstances permit.

There are many different types of hydrographic surveys and beach recons, from simple to complex. The amphibious task force commander who is planning an across-the-beach op will want to know gradient and composition of the beach, littoral

Here and overleaf: A SEAL squad leader and his RTO are an inseparable pair on the battlefield. The radio telephone operator, or RTO, is the team's communication link to fire support from aircraft or tube artillery as well as to the helicopters that will come in to extract the team when the time comes. The team has popped a violet M18 smoke grenade as a recognition signal to the inbound helicopters. These colored grenades are carried by all members of the team and are used for signaling. Some high-concentration white smoke grenades are also sometimes used as an obscurant to screen the squad's movements from enemy eyes.

current across the beach, surf size and type, beach exits, defenses, and obstacles underwater.

It takes a lot of people—or a lot of time—to develop this information. Without getting into the technical details, here's how they do it:

Swim pairs are dropped in the water off the beach at intervals of about twenty-five meters, on line, by a high-speed boat—just like they did fifty years ago out in the Pacific. Under command of the officer in charge (OIC), the swimmers move in toward the beach, making soundings with a lead-line (a lead sinker on a line marked in one-foot increments). While one man measures the depth, the other records the data on a slate. Since all the swimmers make these soundings at the same time, a set of coordinated data is assembled across a wide frontage of possible landing zone.

The line of swimmers moves in to the beach together, with the OIC controlling the intervals between soundings. Both depth and composition are recorded on each swim-pair's slate. The marine task force commander's staff will want to know what they have to contend with. Coral reef? Mud? Jagged rocks? Man-made obstacles with antitank mines attached? Is the fore-shore (the surf zone) too shallow for LSTs, or is it steep and suitable for ramped vessels? Is the surf high and violent or short

An M60 gunner lets loose with a burst; the photograph shows a tracer round leaving the muzzle. Every fifth round in standard belts of machine gun ammo has a small quantity of red phosphorus in the base of the bullet. This material burns for about one second, long enough for the projectile to travel approximately nine hundred meters, or half a mile, and vividly indicates to the gunner the point of impact of his fires.

and mild? Is the current across the beach strong and likely to force the AAMTRACs away from their intended beaches? Then, what's beyond the beach—will tanks and armored vehicles be channeled by sea walls, cliffs, embankments? Are there enemy-prepared fighting positions dominating the beach? Are they manned? Is there a beach patrol? Are there mines?

The survey party moves all the way into the beach and perhaps beyond, then withdraws back to the water. Under the direction of the OIC, they reform a line offshore for pickup. Then, perhaps aboard the flagship for the amphibious task force or wherever the SEAL unit has set up shop, the data from each swim pair is assembled as a detailed chart and presented to the plans-and-operations guys who are trying to figure out what to do. They (through their recommendation to the task force commander) make the call on the amphibious operation, not the SEALs, using the data provided.

There is another kind of recon for which the army and navy SOF communities compete, called *deep recon* or *strategic recon*, and

this one might not involve even getting wet. Deep recon involves the study of a target or area of interest that typically requires covert travel overland or covert insertion inland. SOF teams did this during Desert Shield/Desert Storm in Kuwait and Iraq, watching for enemy SCUD launchers, for example, and reporting their location for attack by other "theater assets" like U.S. Air Force F-15E Strike Eagle aircraft. A SEAL recon team was on the Saudi/Kuwait border when the Iraqis attacked the town of Kafji and participated in the coordinated engagement of the enemy armored column by air and coalition ground units.

HAHO and HALO Insertion

These recon teams can be delivered in some quite exotic ways. One of the sneakiest is by parachute, but SOF teams don't consider the standard 500- or 1,200-foot drop altitude used for mass tactical airborne operations to be very covert; having a C-130 fly low over the neighborhood is one sure way to get noticed. Instead, the drop aircraft goes way up to 30,000 feet or

SEAL squads are sometimes said to be eight men wearing twelve uniforms, and there is certainly a lot of personal choice visible when units are in training for deployment. Each man is permitted great latitude in his choice of load-bearing vest, gloves, headgear, and related battle rattle.

so—where the commercial airliners fly. The jumpers, rigged with special equipment to cope with the incredible cold and the lack of oxygen at that altitude, jump and free fall before deploying their canopies.

The high-altitude exit/high-altitude opening (HAHO) technique allows a jumper to glide for many miles under his canopy, through the dark, virtually without fear of detection, to a predetermined landing zone.

The high-altitude exit/low-opening (HALO) technique is a similar way to have the jumper move away from the ground track of the aircraft, making it difficult to find him. This time, though, the jumper uses free-fall parachuting techniques to fly through the air, opening his canopy only when very close to the ground.

Once down, the mission proceeds as planned. When it is over, one way or another, it is time to go home. While, again, there are many ways to do this, the quickest will again be by aircraft. Unfortunately, though, pickup aircraft are a lot less subtle.

STABO Extraction

An extremely unsubtle extraction technique, stabilized tactical airborne body operations (STABO) involves having a helicopter arrive over the team on the ground with a special harness deployed, coming to a hover, and then plucking the SEALs out of harm's way. The SEALs all wear harnesses similar to those used for parachuting and attach the harnesses to the sling dangling from the helicopter. When all are secured, it's up, up, and away . . . for a very breezy ride.

Strike

The mission against the Panamanian patrol boat was a classic strike or direct-action mission, a carefully planned, precision attack against a point target under difficult circumstances. Using any special ops unit for such an attack is a lot more expensive, in every respect, than using conventional resources to do the

While it has become somewhat fashionable in some communities to wear ball caps with the bill reversed, this SEAL has a very practical reason for wearing his hat this way: it keeps hot cartridge cases from dropping down the back of his neck, and even SEALs don't enjoy being burned that way.

same kind of thing, so there is usually a good reason for sending SEALs to blow the propellers off a boat instead of (for example) having an F/A-18 drop a bomb or smart missile on the target. Collateral damage and loss of life has been one of the driving concerns lately; in Panama, certainly, and in Grenada, too, this caution has created risks of its own.

But ambushes and attacks on point targets are still a major talent of SEALs, another area where they compete with the army's rangers and special forces. These can be conducted in many imaginative ways, most of which are of the high-risk, high-payoff variety (although SEALs sometimes think some of these are high-risk, low-payoff missions).

Ambushes

The ambush is a kind of classic special op mission. SEALs conducted probably thousands of them in Vietnam—and were

on the receiving end of quite a few too. The "plain vanilla" version of the operation works like this: first, find a place where your enemy regularly travels—a road or trail—and find a nice sharp bend in the route. The kill zone will be determined by the patrol leader, normally the long axis of what is an L-shaped portion of the road. The leader will position himself at the corner and will control the whole thing, usually with his own fire and with the triggering of a Claymore mine or two.

Ambushes are marvelously effective when everything works properly—the carnage is *incredible*. But if you screw one up, the carnage can be on your end. And ambushes are easy to screw up; the key is fire discipline and timing. Ambushes don't take a lot of people or a lot of resources (depending on the target, of course), but they do take planning and teamwork.

If available, Claymores are installed along the kill zone with overlapping fields of fire and with careful attention to

During their workup for a combat deployment, a SEAL platoon's members will spend many weeks training with all the unit's authorized weapons, and in the process, each man will expend many thousands of rounds of ammunition. They will conduct drills that come close to simulating some of the conditions of combat—targets appear unexpectedly, stoppages are simulated, shooters have to fire and maneuver quickly. They are firing the M48 medium machine gun here.

protecting the team from the substantial back-blast. If the ambush is along a road, detonation cord can be placed in the ditches that survivors will naturally use for cover after the Claymores fire, and they can be taken out with another squeeze on another clacker, firing the electric blasting cap that will fire the det cord.

When all the preparations are made, the responsibilities and fields of fire assigned, you and the rest of the crew slither into the woodwork without a trace and wait . . . and wait . . . and wait some more. At last, in the distance, somebody is moving toward you; it can be children on their way to school, innocent civilians going to market. You have to sit, silently, waiting for them to pass. What if one of the kids sees the Claymore? What if somebody notices your face peeping out of the brush? Anything that can go wrong, will go wrong to somebody, sooner or later—usually sooner—so it pays to set these things up with exquisite attention to detail.

The way these things are *supposed* to work, an enemy unit will come rolling down the road. With luck (for you, anyway) they will fit the ambush resources; don't pop a Claymore against a platoon of main battle tanks, for example. But if any enemy squad comes bopping down the bunny trail (laughing, playing radios the way they sometimes do), everybody in the ambush waits for the signal to fire. That signal is usually the patrol leader's detonation of the Claymores, hurling their pellets in wide, deadly arcs. If the timing is right and the patrol is within the kill zone, they will all go down—maybe. Some guys are just luckier than others, and fit into a hole in the pattern of the spray of ball bearings. Others may be outside the kill zone. Regardless, this is the time to use all those marksmanship skills they taught you at BUD/S and since. You engage the closest guy with a gun in your field of fire (got a round in the chamber? safety off?), and you keep engaging until there is no more resistance or the patrol leader calls, "Cease fire!" There will be a terrible mess where the patrol was, and this will be a good time to start moving toward the exits.

Ambushes go wrong in lots of ways. Often, the enemy doesn't cooperate. They either won't show up, or they send the wrong victims (like tanks), or they decide not to use the road today, but move along in the woods—where you're hiding. Or they notice you before they get to the kill zone, and then it's *turnabout is fair play*. Then it's your turn to be the victim—and practice those escape-and-evasion skills they taught you in BUD/S. Just remember what they told you at BUD/S: The only easy day was yesterday.

Raids

Raids are quick-in, quick-out strikes against high-value targets that can't be attacked efficiently or effectively otherwise. This is another area where SEALs compete with the army, whose rangers are masters of the art of the raid. Rangers, however, are specialists in the "blunt instrument" style of raid, with lots of people (very large, muscular ones) and lots of firepower landing on top of an enemy target, typically by parachute, and ripping it to shreds.

The SEAL raid is more surgical and subtle. It still might arrive by parachute, but—unlike with our beloved rangers—the enemy target of a SEAL op might never know what hit them. That's because a SEAL strike mission might only involve two men, a sniper and his spotter/security man. With their big .50-caliber sniper rifle and woodcraft skills, these two can move across terrain unseen and disappear into the woodwork. (Rangers attempting this would leave a trail of scorched earth and destruction visible at a mile.) Then the sniper team can sit and wait until the SCUDs come home—and then drill holes in their rocket motors from a mile and a half, without anybody knowing where the bullets came from or how it happened. That same sniper team can, if desired, kill a senior enemy staff officer or commander riding in his Mercedes, pick off a tank commander standing in his hatch, or disable an aircraft taxiing for take-off.

Among the most challenging kind of raid SEALs train for is the counterterrorist hostage rescue mission. This is the kind of op that you only get one shot at; it has to be done perfectly or the wrong folks get killed. Consequently SEALs practice all the ancient arts of rapid insertion, extraction, close-quarters target identification, and precision shooting. According to people who've been there, you've got seven seconds in a room with the bad guys to conduct business—sort out the good from the bad, kill the bad guys, protect the good guys—or the operation goes to hell. When you consider that this must often be done at night, in unfamiliar territory, with alert and fanatic enemies, this becomes a tall order. But it can be done, and has, successfully.

Killing People and Destroying Things

A sad but unavoidable consequence of all military missions involves taking perfectly good buildings, airplanes, vehicles, bridges, boats, and people, then taking them apart and converting them into smaller, less useful junk. This process is generally thought to help accomplish national policy objectives. While this behavior isn't always considered very nice, it usually works. This is conflict resolution, U.S. Navy SEALs style.

There are many ways SEALs accomplish their missions, but basically there are only two fundamental techniques used by the teams. One of these uses individual weapons—rifles, machine guns, mortars—to engage other hostile forces. The other involves using explosives in one form or another to blow things up. "Hostile forces" is a military expression for the loyal soldiers or sailors opposing the SEAL mission, and "engage" is a military expression for the business of shooting up these folks in an organized way. If this seems like kindergarten, it is only because we generally talk around the seamier side of the business of war.

SEAL missions often involve the destruction of some enemy facility—a radio transmitter, a bridge, a bunker complex, a headquarters, or (as in the attack on the *Presidente Porras* in the beginning of this book) a naval vessel. This usually involves the use of high explosives in one of many forms, and one thing most SEALs quickly discover in BUD/S is that explosives are *fun*. As one blaster says with a smirk, "There are very few of life's troubles that can't be cured with high explosives."

A Short Course in Demolitions and High Explosives

Despite what you hear, high explosives are quite safe to handle and are actually difficult to detonate. Most of the military varieties can be pounded with a hammer (old, runny dynamite excepted) without going off. One of the best materials for blasting passages through coral reefs is a simple mixture of fertilizer and diesel fuel. You can break off a chunk of TNT from a quarter-pound block and set fire to it; so it's not only a great explosive, it's also a great heat source for warming up your lunch. C4, the famous "plastic explosive," looks, feels, and acts like putty—a white material that you can easily form and shape with your fingers, in complete safety. The same is true of virtually all other military explosives, with the possible exception of dynamite, a combination of nitroglycerine and gun-cotton that can become quite unstable if stored improperly. Most of these materials can sit on the shelf for decades without any significant decay, and it isn't unusual to be issued cratering charges, for example, that were made during World War II.

For these and other reasons, explosives are very interesting and useful materials, available in many forms. There is Primacord, or det cord, a material that looks like fuse, a flexible plastic-like quarter-inch cord that contains a very high explosive, PETN, and is used to connect main charges. The PETN cord is set off with a blasting cap or other charge—then it explodes at a linear rate of about four miles per second with enough force

to detonate any U.S. military explosive the cord is tied to. It is very handy stuff for making a lot of little charges all go off at the same time—and other, sneakier applications discussed later.

In every case, including that of dynamite, you must work hard and carefully to actually get the stuff to go off. And that's accomplished with a little device that is quite dangerous and that will go off if you fail to handle it with care, caution, and respect—the blasting cap. These come in two flavors: electric and fused. Both are tubes of aluminum or copper, a quarter of an inch in diameter, partially filled with a three-stage mixture of specialized explosives, an ignition charge, a priming charge, and a base charge. Although things happen quickly, these charges go off in sequence, and the last one, the base charge, is the one that *should* set off the main charge.

As an example, let's set off a one-pound block of TNT. The main charge comes in a cardboard tube with a threaded receptacle on the ends to hold the blasting cap. We'll use common fuse instead of an electrical cap for this charge; it's more traditional—also less safe.

First we take the fuse, cut six inches off the end and discard it. This should remove any contaminated and unreliable material. Then we cut a section six feet long, light one end, and time the delay. After about four minutes, a little flash of fire will come from the end. Note the time (in seconds), divide by six, and you know what the delay of the fuse is in seconds per foot; normally it is about forty seconds per foot. Now, using your combination tool designed for demolitions work, cut a good, healthy length of fuse sufficient for five minutes of delay. The ends should be clean, square cuts.

Remove a blasting cap from the storage box where they are kept for safety and inspect the fuse well for foreign matter. *Gently* slip the fuse into the open end—about an inch—and into contact with the ignition charge. Crimp the fuse to the cap with the crimper part of the tool, about a quarter inch from the end of the cap. Now gently insert the cap into the priming well of the TNT block, place it on the ground, and extend the fuse so that it doesn't coil over on itself. We could use a fuse-lighter to get things started, but you might as well learn the traditional way first: split the fuse end about half an inch, insert a match head in the core, and strike it. The match will ignite the black powder inside, a bit of flame will sputter, a little smoke will be emitted, and it is time to vacate the premises. It is considered good manners to shout, "Fire in the hole!" at this point unless there are bad guys in the vicinity. You walk, not run, well away, take cover, note the time, and await developments.

It's amazing what you can do to trick out the basic M4 carbine variant of the venerable M16 rifle. SEALs always have a PEQ-4 laser pointer/illuminator on their weapons. Also installed will be an optical sight and probably an M203 40mm grenade launcher, all attached to the weapon on a so-called Picatinny rail system. The standard collapsible stock has also been replaced by an upgraded version, and it is also now common for SEALs to use painted camouflage on their weapons.

Two members of a SEAL squad chat before being sent down a path in the underbrush to engage targets and avoid booby-traps.

at the same instant, and a small amount of explosive (a pound and a half per foot of thickness) will crumble the concrete.

The most common application of explosives for SEALs has been clearing beach obstacles prior to amphibious landings, a technique developed to a minor art form by the UDT swimmers during World War II and Korea. Besides that use, vast quantities of C4 went up in smoke in Vietnam and, more recently, in the Gulf, blowing up bunkers and creating diversions. You can make a foxhole in a hurry with it, crater a road, cut a railroad line or a thick telephone cable. In the form of a Bangalore torpedo (a long section of steel pipe filled with explosive) you can blast a gap through a barbed wire obstacle or a minefield. It is mighty handy stuff.

Det cord, all by itself, has an interesting application for those occasional ambushes where you have plenty of time to set up shop. It can be electrically primed and hidden in roadside ditches alongside the kill zone. When the ambush is initiated, you can be reasonably certain that the survivors of the first blast of small arms fire will dive for the presumed protection of the handy ditch. If the SEAL with the "hell box" (as the blasting machine is called) remembers to twist the handle about now, the "det" cord will explode in the ditch, adding to the consternation and woe of the enemy force.

Claymore Mines

The Claymore mine was developed in Vietnam to deal with those nasty situations when a couple of hundred little fellers in black pajamas were swarming across the barbed wire defenses of a compound with intentions of committing mayhem on the residents. The Claymore is a simple little package of C4 explosive and a few hundred steel ball bearings, fired with an electric blasting cap and a "clacker" (a one-handed electric generator that, when squeezed, will fire the cap). When the explosive detonates, the ball bearings spray a wide area with deadly effect, usually helping to convince the enemy force that there may be other, better, things to do than to attack this particular place.

Claymores have since become favorites for temporary defensive fighting positions and for ambushes, where they excel. Like virtually all other weapons, they are not perfect or foolproof. One sneaky trick the VC learned was to find them and turn them around.

The guy with the clacker in an ambush setup has to be a very cool dude, sufficiently self-disciplined to wait until the enemy is properly within the kill zone before firing the weapon. Lots of perfectly good ambushes have been ruined by the premature

When the fuse burns down inside a non-electric blasting cap, a little squirt of flame shoots out, into the cap. If everything works as planned, the ignition charge goes off, then the priming charge, which detonates the base charge of the cap, and that little blast will usually set off the TNT. There will be a loud *Boom!*, and dust and rocks will scatter for a hundred meters in all directions. But don't expect any gaping crater—even a pound of TNT won't do much unless it is artfully placed and prepared. Instead, we have a patch of ground that is lightly depressed and not much more.

Explosives are used to do very specific things and are used with mathematical precision. You can cut a twelve-inch-diameter tree with a half-pound block and have it fall across a roadway, blocking traffic. You can make a ribbon out of C4 plastic explosive, stick it to a steel girder, and cut a bridge support. You can shape it into a flat diamond and wrap it around an eighteen-inch-diameter ship's propeller shaft, prime both points with blasting caps, and cut off the shaft neatly when the charge goes off. Put two identical charges on both sides of a concrete wall or abutment and prime electrically so both go off

Here and overleaf: This squad is conducting GOPLATS take-down drills by fast-rope insertion from an SH-60 Sea Hawk helicopter. Oil platforms typically have helipads so this ought to be a simple procedure, but gas and oil platforms in the Persian Gulf have sometimes been heavily fortified against such assaults. Even without such precautions, these platforms are inherently dangerous places, loaded with hot, high-pressure, explosive gasses and liquids. They are also noisy, and have oil-coated decks that make footing uncertain. Real-world GOPLATS take-downs are conducted at night.

detonation of the Claymore, removing the element of surprise quickly and completely.

SEALs carry a Claymore or two along on some of their excursions, the whole kit of mine, clacker, wire, and blasting cap all stored neatly in a little bundle complete with carrying strap.

.50-Caliber Sniper Rifle

One fine, somewhat neglected military art is that of the sniper. SEALs and Green Berets study this skill at the target interdiction course, part of the Special Operations Command Center and School at the Fort Bragg, North Carolina. Here, out among the weeds and chiggers, apprentice SEAL snipers learn how to move invisibly across any terrain, to build a hide so natural that an enemy can stand on top of it and not know that two navy

SEALs are in residence below, and to shoot so well that enemy soldiers over a half mile away die with the first shot, tank commanders standing in the turrets of their tanks lose their heads (literally), and antennas and vision ports on armored vehicles become useless.

The key to all this is a relatively simple, relatively ancient weapon—the rifle. The one favored by special operators like the SEALs these days is the big .50-caliber single-shot, bolt-action model that weighs about twenty pounds with scope and bipod. For a variety of reasons the big half-inch bullet will fly very accurately, very far. It will reliably strike a man-sized target so far away that the noise from its firing is practically inaudible, out to ranges of two kilometers, more than a mile and a half. But to achieve such accuracy requires far more than just an accurate

weapon and sights. A SEAL sniper team out in the bush must deal with wind, moving targets, slant angles, and heat distortion.

Snipers work as two-man teams: the shooter and the spotter. They are inserted near their objective by boat or parachute, or swim ashore from a submarine, or come by Volkswagen bus—whatever works for the tactical situation. They will travel the last kilometer or so to their hide by crawling. It can take a day or more.

Their weapons and equipment are contained in a "drag bag," pulled along behind each. Under cover of darkness, they carefully, methodically carve a hole in the ground, then re-cover it so artfully that it seems perfectly undisturbed. In this hole the pair will live for a day or two, observing, recording, and possibly reporting by radio. Normally the sniper's mission will not include actually firing on an enemy force but calling in artillery or aviation to do the job.

Determining range to the target and wind effect are the two principal problems confronting the sniper team, and the pair will expend considerable effort preparing to fire the first shot. A big .50-caliber round is inserted into the breech, the bolt brought forward, locked, and the sights carefully aligned on a computed aim point.

The spotter uses a compact telescope to look downrange. Instead of watching the target, the spotter watches for the *bullet* as it streaks toward the victim. With proper training and the right weather conditions, you can actually see a bullet and the vapor trail produced as it flies through the atmosphere. The spotter reports the point of impact to the shooter for any corrections.

Chapter 6

SPECIAL BOAT SQUADRONS— THE BROWN WATER NAVY

The 11-meter RIB is one of the essential items in the inventory of a SEAL team conducting operations in a maritime environment today. Several versions are used but the 11-meter model will carry a complete squad of eight men and their gear at high speed and relative safety. The hull is a type of fiberglass and offers stiffness and strength. The buoyancy tubes make the RIB unsinkable in any sea state and allow tight turns at speed. A crew of three SBS members is assigned to RIBs. The boats are equipped with radar, radios, M2HB machine guns, and Mk19 grenade launchers. The larger of these RIBs is good for better than thirty-five knots/40 miles per hour and has a rated range of two hundred nautical miles. That means a squad can launch from a ship well over the horizon and zoom across the waves to take down an oil platform or other target with a minimal chance of detection.
Eric Logsdon, U.S. Navy SPECWARCOM

s mentioned earlier, the SBSs have typically been somewhat neglected in favor of the higher profile SEAL teams in the development of NSW. That's too bad because the boats have as rich a combat history as the teams, and both have worked closely together for nearly three decades. In fact, one of the big selling points for NSW in the competitive business of special operations is the unique resource SPECWARCOM has in its fleet of boats designed to take the fight close to the beach and up all those lazy rivers.

The SBSs are teamed with the SEALs to provide a kind of mutual support. And, just as the SEALs have a variety of weapons to choose from for their missions, the SBS crews have a menu of boats as well. There are little IBS inflatables, RIBs, PBRs, and fast-attack patrol boats. Most are stunningly fast, with thirty-knot-plus speeds—although you only get speeds like that from an IBS (a little seven-man rubber duck) when all the BUD/S are screaming and the students are paddling like crazy.

Mission mobility for NSW provides an extremely diverse set of problems for the "Coronado Yacht Club." The three basic areas of responsibility for the SBS part of NSW are coastal patrol and interdiction, special operations mission support, and riverine patrol and interdiction. But don't think that there's a sharp line between any of these assignments—the real world has a way of mixing and matching them. The boat that is primarily intended for coastal patrol may find itself occasionally on a riverine mission, or executing some exotic special operations support assignment.

Specifically intended for river operations, the SOC-R is crewed by four men from the SBS and provides express taxi service for six SEALs and their combat equipment. Twin diesel engines drive Jacuzzi pumps that propel the boat at speeds up to about thirty-five knots/forty miles per hour. The SOC-R is based on extensive battle experience in the Mekong Delta during the war in Vietnam and Southeast Asia. One of those lessons is that it pays to go in heavily armed and armored, so the boats have M2HB .50-caliber machine guns and Mk19s, as well as ceramic armor kits for the vital areas of the vessel.

Eric Logsdon, U.S. Navy SPECWARCOM

Are we having fun yet? Even on small rivers and crowded estuaries in the middle of the night, the SOC-R's crew can jam along at high speed and relative safety thanks to the boat's shallow draft, excellent radar, and tremendous agility. The SEAL passengers ride in comparative comfort without the pounding that comes with high-speed offshore missions. *Eric Logsdon, U.S. Navy SPECWARCOM*

Coastal Patrol and Interdiction

The first of these, requiring the biggest vessels, is the coastal patrol mission. The offshore patrol and interdiction mission is very different than, say, the clandestine insertion of a couple of combat swimmers for a demolition raid. It takes a good-sized vessel to provide the kind of platform needed to stay offshore for very long, to provide reasonable comfort for the crew, and to have the speed and firepower to accomplish anything useful. These missions are currently assigned to the patrol boat, coastal (PBC), Mk III swift patrol boat, and the Mk IV patrol boat.

Neither the PBR or PBL (patrol boat, light) provide much speed or comfort out past the surf zone; they're flat water boats with a specific set of missions. For the offshore jobs, where the Sea State goes up to five or so and the waves swell up to twelve feet, even froggy SEALs want something sturdy and stable. That pretty well eliminates the light little flat-bottomed boats in favor of something longer and beamier, with a nice, sharp V-hull to slide through the waves instead of pound along on top of them.

Patrol Boat, Coastal

The PBC is something of a major change for the NSW community—the introduction of an entirely new class of ship to support NAVSPECWARCOM missions. In the past such support has been improvised, based on whatever happens to be around. The PC-1 class formalizes the support.

Ships of this class, starting with the *Cyclone* (PC-1), are designed for serious patrol work, their primary mission. NSW support is secondary, but a dedicated assignment. With an overall length of 170 feet, the PBCs are big enough for serious offshore work, reasonably comfortable, and commodious enough for a rather large number of embarked SEALs and NSW players.

The ships are the biggest platform the SBSs have ever had. They're funded by SOCOM and are assigned to the NSW groups at Coronado and Little River, but are likely to be forward based. There will be a total of thirteen of the PBCs when the program is complete.

A SEAL relaxes before his CRRC gets underway.

Obviously, it is hard to be very covert with 170 feet of warship. Rather than sneaking and peeking like the little boats, the PBCs will be used to "show the flag" while maintaining a U.S. presence in regions where the national command authority wants a show of force. The ships will be tasked with monitoring and detection missions, escort operations, noncombatant evacuation, and foreign internal defense—all pretty much the plain-vanilla patrol mission assigned to any of the navy's or coast guard's smaller ships.

The more interesting missions, and the ones the NSW community is involved in, are for long-range insertion and extraction of SEAL teams, tactical-swimmer operations, intelligence collection, operational deception, and coastal or riverine support.

The PBC's steel hull with aluminum superstructure has a beam of twenty-five feet and a draft of about eight feet; it displaces about 330 tons (full load). Propulsion comes from twin diesels that can drive the ship at thirty-five knots. A tank of fuel (about thirteen thousand gallons) will give a range of about two thousand nautical miles at a moderate cruise speed of twelve knots. The ship will tolerate Sea State 5 conditions—rough sea with waves of eight to twelve feet. There is a platform on the stern for launching and recovering combat swimmers and the ships each have two CRRCs available for SEAL operations.

Normal complement is four officers and twenty-four enlisted personnel. Unlike previous SBS vessels, the commander of the PBC ships is not likely to be a SEAL but a surface warfare officer. While there is some apprehension about this, there is also the realization that this is an entirely new asset for the community, with a somewhat different mission; and how it all works out remains to be seen. There will probably be at least a few SEALs assigned. Besides the crew, there is berthing for a nine-man SOF or law-enforcement detachment aboard.

Appropriate to its size and missions, the PCs will be the most heavily armed of NSW craft. A Mk 38 25mm rapid-fire gun is installed, along with a station for the Stinger antiaircraft missile system. Four mounts for heavy automatic weapons are available for the Mk 19 40mm grenade launcher, the M2 .50-caliber machine gun, and the M60 7.62mm machine gun. For antiship missile defense, a Mk 52 chaff/decoy system is installed.

Mk III Swift Patrol Boat

The Mk III is a big, sixty-five-foot boat designed back in the 1960s with a coastal mission in mind. These boats have been used extensively in combat over the years, particularly to patrol the waters off the coast of Vietnam and, more recently, the Latin American coastal waters used by drug traffickers and the Persian Gulf waters in support of Desert Storm. The basic mission is to serve as a high-speed weapons platform for NSW units. The deck is reinforced to tolerate recoil stresses from the many weapons that can be mounted on the Mk III—any mix of 20mm cannon, 81mm or 60mm mortar, Mk 19 40mm grenade launcher, .50-caliber machine gun, and the faithful old M60 7.62mm machine gun.

The boat is rated at thirty-plus knots, needs a crew of eleven, and can stay out up to five days. It is powered by three big diesel engines installed in an all-aluminum hull with a low-profile radar and acoustic signature (for this kind of boat, anyway) that makes it comparatively easy to accomplish some kinds of covert missions. The navy will tell you officially that it is "reasonably" stable in "moderately" heavy seas, but most experienced offshore operators will tell you that a sixty-five-foot hull fits neatly in the troughs of most any sea and will wallow like a pig in mud given half an opportunity.

But NSW boats aren't intended to be pleasure craft. The Mk III is tasked with patrol and interdiction missions, with fire-support missions against targets ashore or afloat, and the insertion of SEAL team elements. One of their users, an SBS unit commander, says of them, "They've lasted through everything we've sent them to, from Vietnam to the Persian Gulf—and in fact the Persian Gulf is where they've gotten their heaviest workout." The Mk III is an old boat now, nearing retirement. An improved model, the Mk IV, is in service, but a completely new version, to be called the Mk V, is in the long design and acquisition process.

Mk IV Patrol Boat

The Sea Spectre sixty-eight-foot patrol boat is an improved version of the Mk III, an evolution of a proven design with some substantial upgrades. The missions, specifications, and weapons remain about the same, but the boat is designed to be more easily adaptable to the wide variety of missions that such boats are tasked for. Like its older brother, it is not a heavy weather offshore boat (that doesn't mean you don't have to operate in those conditions, just that you'll be uncomfortable when you do).

Special Operations Support Mission

Support for special operations doesn't have the same kind of requirements for station time that patrol does, and the boats used for inserting and supporting SEALs and other SOC

Here and overleaf: Although SEALs and SBSs use inflatable
boats from many manufacturers and models, the classic
for many years has been Zodiac's little F-470, a French
import that is popular with all U.S. SOF. It's only about 15.5
feet long but is stable and fast when not heavily loaded. It
is one of the few boats that can be launched from a
submerged submarine for very covert insertions. It is an
over-the-horizon insertion platform but no longer the first
choice for such missions because of the F-470s limited
payload and sea-keeping qualities. But it is the only boat in
the inventory that can be brought ashore, deflated, and
buried while the SEALs are busy with their mission. Unlike
the RIBs, the F-470 may be propelled by an engine or
paddles, the latter for a virtually silent approach to a
hostile shore. A whole squad of eight men can be carried,
but that's really pushing the capacity of the boat.

operators are designed with things other than comfort in mind: speed, range, capacity, and a low radar signature are far more important than stability or fuel economy.

And the SBS crews and boats aren't always supporting strictly SEALs or NSW personnel; part of the idea of the joint SOF when it was established was to coordinate and integrate all the operators going downrange. So these SBS and NSW assets give rides to Green Berets and Rangers as well as to SEALs, and even to the occasional Force Recon Marine.

Rigid Inflatable Boats

Rigid inflatable boats (RIBs) are the boat of the hour. Everybody's making and using them. Pretty soon you'll probably

be able to take a Caribbean cruise on one. They're simple, cheap, fairly economical, and faster than a speeding bullet. They are used by the navy, the coast guard, and many foreign nations. They combine some of the best features of rigid hull and inflatable designs in one fast, stable, buoyant platform.

There are three variants of the big rubber duck used by the SEALs: twenty-four-foot, thirty-foot, and ten-meter RIBs. All use fiberglass hulls with a V-shaped cross section, offering stability, a rigid motor mount, and firm footing, along with an inflatable gunwale section. The inflatable part of the boat is fabricated from an extremely tough material, a combination of hypalon neoprene and nylon reinforced fabric. It won't shed bullets, but it will take a lot of lesser abuse, including the pounding you get from jamming

around offshore, punching through the waves. The hammering a boat takes in normal service can be pretty severe, cracking fiberglass and aluminum hulls with the constant flexing. That is not a problem with an inflatable.

The RIBs are extremely tolerant, for a small boat, of heavy seas. With light loads the boats have operated offshore in extreme conditions—the Sea State 6 and winds of forty-five knots. That means waves up to twenty feet high, when even SEALs would rather be ashore, even at BUD/S. While the boats can operate in such conditions, they normally don't go out when things get that bad; the SOP calls for a Sea State

5/thirty-four-knot wind limit on use. All the boats are normally crewed by three SBS sailors.

The twenty-four-foot RIB weighs in at about ten thousand pounds fully loaded. It is powered by a single Volvo inboard engine/outboard drive powerplant and has a rated maximum speed of twenty-eight knots. Range is 175 nautical miles at twenty-five-knot speeds. Even this little boat mounts a radar—and an M60 7.62mm machine gun. Its principal mission is to deliver a single SEAL fire team (half a squad, four men) to an insertion point. It isn't the stealthiest way to insert a SEAL element on a covert mission, but not all missions require invisibility.

The thirty-foot RIB is quite similar to the twenty-four-foot version, but with two engines driving water jet drives and a higher rated maximum speed of thirty-two knots. The thirty-footer is, as a result, half again heavier, weighing in at a combat weight of about fifteen thousand pounds. Range is slightly less, at 150 nautical miles, and the payload is a bit bigger.

The biggest of the breed is the ten-meter (thirty-three-foot) inflatable. This one will accommodate a whole squad. This means that an entire eight-man SEAL combat element can be cold, wet, and miserable while they huddle behind the dubious armor of two thin sheets of high-tech rubber and about two feet of compressed air on the run in to that hostile shore. The boat can be pumped up to forty knots, just in case the coxswain decides to race an aircraft carrier or perhaps outflank the fleet. And when he gets in range, this inflatable warship carries two weapons mounts accommodating either M60s or Mk 19 grenade launchers. There's enough fuel aboard for about an eight-hour mission, providing a range of around 250 nautical miles.

Combat Rubber Raiding Craft

One of the most used and useful boats in the inventory is a kind of war-surplus model left over from World War II, the combat rubber raiding craft (CRRC)—the legendary little rubber duck. Originally designed as a life raft, the boat has been adopted and adapted to all sorts of offensive missions. Marines use it, Rangers and Green Berets use it, and of course the SEALs use it, for clandestine surface insertions and extractions. The CRRC weighs only 265 pounds. It gets tossed out of C-130 airplanes or from cargo helicopters, along with the SEALs, into the ocean. It is also launched from submarines, either from the surface or submerged, or gets chucked over the side of larger surface craft.

It's only about fifteen feet long, with a six-foot beam, but it will do about twenty knots. That, of course, requires an outboard engine, a single fifty-five horsepower powerplant with an eighteen-gallon fuel bladder providing a range of about sixty-five miles. That offers over-the-horizon capability, but—trust me on this—you don't want to ride one in to the beach from over the horizon except on the *nicest* of days.

It is an extremely versatile piece of gear. While civilians spend hundreds or thousands of dollars on health clubs and Nordic Track exercise machines, the Navy uses the CRRC at BUD/S to build better bodies eight ways. In fact, the BUD/S instructors have discovered that you don't need fancy machines or chrome-plated weights, just a CRRC; if you have the students

hold one overhead for a few minutes it *really* works those upper-body muscles. And, for a little extra help for those who need it, the CRRC can easily hold plenty of wet sand, bringing its weight up to something more challenging.

The inflatables have another virtue lacking in most other Navy property: they are, at times, considered disposable. Rather than go through the time and trouble to bring one back aboard a submerged sub, you may, during real world combat operations, stick your dive knife into one when you're done with your mission and let it sink to the bottom, engine and all. Just make sure that the submarine is standing by for you first!

Swimmer Delivery Vehicle Mk VIII

Perhaps the most interesting, least publicized, most covert boat the NSW community operates is the wet submersible called the swimmer delivery vehicle (SDV) Mk VIII. It's an odd little submarine SEALs use for fast, covert subsurface insertions. The SDV is like a little speed boat, with rechargeable batteries and an electric motor for propulsion. Like other submarines, the SDV is visually blind and relies on sensors and instrumentation to navigate without bumping into things.

The embarked SEALs climb into a fully enclosed cabin. Although they wear scuba or closed-circuit breathing systems for backup and for work outside the vehicle, the SDV has its own supply of breathing air.

SDVs are launched from surface craft sometimes, but the dry deck shelter (DDS) attached to a submarine is a more typical point of departure. The DDS is like a small hangar, big enough for the SDV and with enough room for the swimmers to enter from the sub and climb into the SDV. The DDS is gradually flooded, the hatch opened, and out goes the SDV in search of adventure. The divers are now essentially in an expensive tin can full of water. It can be a cold ride. As one of its users says:

"It's a strange ride. You can't see out. You fly on instruments the entire time. You are a diver the entire time you're in it. The SDV provides more speed and range than swimming. Quite honestly, the boat will go farther than the man will. Exposure to the cold and to the ambient sea pressure put tremendous strains on the human body that become a limiting factor for missions with SDV. I don't think it's used enough, perhaps because its reliability hasn't always been too great. It is a complicated thing to support and deliver. But if you plan its use properly, if you get it within its range, it is an extremely effective tool because it is almost nondetectable. The ability to deliver either SEALs or ordnance is just phenomenal!"

The vehicle has its own support unit, the SDV team, within SPECWARCOM. These teams maintain and operate the SDV, SEALs who actually man the boats on missions. An operator and a navigator are always assigned; both are fully qualified SEALs who have what amounts to a kind of bus driver job in addition to the usual combat assignments in the objective area.

The SDV is rated to carry six swimmers and their equipment, including the crew of two. A sonar sensor (for object avoidance) and an inertial navigation system allow the operator to cruise around underwater. A third sensor system is sometimes installed as part of a developmental program, but that remains "buggy," a side-scanning sonar for target identification of objects like mines as well as to record bottom contour. Not too surprisingly, a lot of specific performance information about these exotic little boats is classified. While the specifics are secret, we are authorized to hint a lot: The vehicle is about twice as fast as a submerged swimmer; vehicle endurance is probably a lot longer than crew endurance; and the SDV will tolerate up to five hundred feet of water pressure without failing, and that's a lot farther than the crew will go before their sub-systems start to fail! We could tell you more, but then we'd have to kill you.

Actually, though, the whole vehicle was extremely classified for a very long time. It couldn't be moved without being covered, and of course no photographs could be released showing it. But a few years ago, the then commander of SPECWARCOM decided the SDV would be a nice addition to the unit's annual float in the Coronado Fourth of July parade and ordered it displayed on the flatbed trailer, along with the usual "cammied" Naval SPECWARCOM warriors. That's the way it is sometimes around NSW—things that are super-secret on one day and in one place are proudly displayed to the world the next.

Riverine Patrol and Interdiction

SEAL experience in Vietnam strongly demonstrated the need for good shallow-draft boats with plenty of speed, stealth, space for combat-equipped SEALs, and provisions for both defending and attacking when in contact with enemy forces. That mission still exists today, in Latin America, where the United States is involved in a quiet war in the backwaters of the Amazon basin and elsewhere. The boats from that previous war, along with some new ones, are helping to fight this one. Sometimes SEALs are embarked, sometimes not. In some cases the operators are foreign military or law enforcement people who are equipped and trained by the United States, often by SEALs in the Foreign Internal Defense mission.

Patrol Boat, River

The patrol boat, river (PBR) has been around since quite early in the Vietnam War. It is still serving long after most of its crews have retired, a design with an interesting history.

When SEAL Team One packed its bags and shipped out to the combat zone in 1966 it was pretty much without a really good boat to support its new missions. Existing navy Landing Craft, Personnel, Launch (LCPL) fleet craft had been modified for the purpose but just didn't seem suitable for the riverine mission of fast, long-range, shallow-draft patrol. That's why, in September 1965, the Navy's Bureau of Ships published a request for bids on a twenty-five to thirty-knot boat with a "dead-in-the-water" draft of eighteen inches and a draft at speed of only nine inches. A slightly modified commercial design from the Hattaras Yacht Company was selected, a twenty-eight-foot boat with Jacuzzi-type propulsion.

The prototype was delivered only two weeks later. After testing, the design was modified, lengthened a bit to thirty-one feet, and christened the PBR Mk I. The boats were being delivered to the navy only a year after the program began. Not much later they were zooming around the Mekong Delta, trading shots with the VC and providing a kind of taxi service for SEALs off on nocturnal excursions.

The PBR was designed for high-speed patrol and insertion operations in rivers and bays. It is a heavily armed and armored boat, designed for combat at close quarters, with special ceramic armor similar to that used on tanks applied to the vessels' crew compartment. The hull is made of thick, reinforced fiberglass and is designed to accept the stresses of recoiling heavy machine guns and grenade launchers. The current PBR in service is thirty-two feet long, with a beam of about twelve feet. It weighs about eighteen thousand pounds, light enough to be transported on C-5 Galaxy aircraft.

While fairly ancient as military systems go, it is still an amazing boat. The two big General Electric diesel engines will tootle along quietly or crank up 215 horsepower each when required. Those engines each drive a fourteen-inch Jacuzzi pump; the water squirts out of 5.75-inch nozzles, making the boat go faster than thirty knots—in excess of thirty-five miles an hour to you landlubbers. Of course, that's with the water jets clean, and they do clog up. It has a range of two hundred miles on 160 gallons of fuel. Normal crew complement is four.

A lot of bullets have dinged off the hulls and armor of PBRs, and a lot of crewmen have died aboard them. The boats have done a lot of shooting of their own. Standard equipment includes a tub-mounted twin M2 .50-caliber machine gun system in the bow; that's industrial-strength firepower guaranteed to "clean the clock" of almost any point target within two kilometers. There is also a pedestal mount for another M2 .50-caliber and a mount for the marvelous Mk 19 grenade launcher, a type of machine gun that fires 40mm, baseball-sized projectiles to better than two kilometers. As options you can sometimes get a 60mm mortar installed, with or without M60 machine guns, and additional .50-caliber and 40mm machine guns mounted amidship. Of the more than five hundred PBRs built since 1966 only twenty-four or so remain in service. A new design is in the works.

Patrol Boat, Light

The patrol boat, light (PBL) is another modified off-the-shelf civilian design from that distant era; still in use is the twenty-five-foot military version of the Boston Whaler, an unsinkable little boat powered by a pair of big engines and mounting two heavy weapons, the M2 .50-caliber machine gun and/or the Mk 19 grenade launcher. The PBL is a light, fast, air-portable, quiet, somewhat vulnerable boat that has evolved a bit over the years but continues to support the riverine mission after almost three decades in the inventory.

Like the PBR, it uses water-jet propulsion to achieve better than thirty-knot speeds on flat water. It will turn on a proverbial dime—in fact, the boat will turn a lot faster than the coxswain and crew will probably find comfortable, a 180-degree about-face in less than thirty feet while doing thirty knots. While the g-load of such a maneuver could easily toss most everybody right out of the boat, it is a handy capability for those times you come blasting around a bend and find a horde of bad guys waiting for your arrival.

Two pedestal-mounted "Ma Duce" heavy machine guns are mounted just forward of the coxswain's position. This provides all-aspect firepower for breaking contact when the crew of three thinks it is necessary. There is also a third mount farther forward, and any combination of .50-caliber and 7.62mm machine guns can be installed.

Although the PBL draws about a foot and a half of water when stopped, at speed it will just about operate in a mud puddle, skimming along on the surface of the water rather than through it. The two engines will run at full throttle for eight hours on a tank of fuel, driving the boat across about 160 nautical miles of river or canal at more than twenty-five knots. It uses standard twin engines, with dual steerage, ignition, and controls for backup redundancy.

It is an extremely mobile little boat, in and out of the water. The PBL can travel on a conventional trailer, be rigged as a sling load for a helicopter, or be loaded aboard a C-130. A lot of PBLs have traveled to Latin American military forces, where they are justifiably popular with the counter-narcotics forces patrolling the Amazon delta and other riverine battlefields.

Mini-Armored Troop Carrier

The mini-armored troop carrier (MATC) is a kind of small landing craft similar to the ones marines have been using to come ashore for decades, only smaller. It has a flat, ramp-type bow that drops forward to eject a whole platoon of sixteen combat-equipped SEALs onto a beach. It is a riverine craft with shallow draft and all the sea-keeping qualities of a cork. Like the PBR and most other riverine craft, the MATC has a water-jet propulsion system that "vacuums" the boat through the water, Jacuzzi fashion. A crew of three operates the boat.

Its hull is thirty-six feet long, made of aluminum, and is designed for high-speed patrol, interdiction, and combat assault missions on the relatively flat waters of bays, rivers, canals, and protected coastal areas. It is serious about all this—there are seven weapons stations for heavy machine guns or grenade launchers and a 60mm mortar can be installed. It comes with a high-resolution radar and a rack of radios for every taste and purpose. The boat weighs about twenty-five thousand pounds, is good for about thirty knots and a range of 230 nautical miles from 430 gallons of fuel.

In the grand SEAL tradition, the boat is fast and sneaky. It has a low six-foot profile that's hard to see or pick up on radar (well, for a slab-sided metal-hulled boat). The engines are extremely quiet. What this all means is that you can pile a bunch of weapons and troops aboard, run up the river to a likely spot, slide into the weeds and woodwork along the bank, and wait, engine at idle. With good comms you can talk to surveillance aircraft overhead, other teams ashore and afloat in the area, and wait for your victim to come chugging down the creek. When the perpetrators of the crime arrive on scene, the MATC has the troops and the firepower to negotiate with just about anybody and win through intimidation.

RIBs have become popular with the NSW community because the rigid hull eliminates the problem of flexing that limits the conventional inflatables like the F-470. The stiffening allows much higher speeds and guaranteed buoyancy offshore in conditions up to Sea State 5 or 6 (waves eighteen feet high, winds to about thirty knots).

Chapter 7

LEADER'S RECON

Before a combat operation, particularly ashore, a commander will, time permitting, travel to the objective area for eyes on the target, as Lieutenant Tom Dietz did before the diversionary raid on the Iraqi coastal defenses in Kuwait. This personal study by a combat commander of an area where conflict will occur is called "leader's recon." There is no good substitute for this kind of personal, direct contact by the combat leader with the battlefield. For people within military communities there are all kinds of battlefields besides the kind we usually think of. Some are institutional, within the unit, while others are the political, doctrinal, policy arenas. For the past fifty years, SEALs have had to adapt to changes in the world, in the U.S. armed forces, in the navy, and within NSW itself. These internal battles shape the nature of the institution that will fight the wars of the future. These institutional, peacetime conflicts are tremendously dangerous—not for the present, but for the time when push comes to shove, as it always seems to do.

Among the most dangerous things SEALs need to worry about is complacency on their own part, about bad tactical habits, about inexperience and overconfidence. Despite several combat operations over the last couple of decades, the SEAL community today is almost completely inexperienced in war—and this is a dangerous thing. War is different than training, no matter how tough that training may be.

Combat experience is slipping away from the navy. The last Navy Medal of Honor winner retired in 1992, and nearly all the Vietnam combat veterans have left the formal military service. One of these men with a great deal of combat time is Commander Gary Stubblefield, recently retired but still actively working with NSW as a consultant and contractor. With retirement comes a greater freedom to discuss NSW issues. The following are a kind of leader's recon offered by Stubblefield, a selection of opinions and insights about the life and times of SEALs today and in the future. His observations are a rare insight into the challenges of the present and future for NSW.

(Continued on page 118)

The SEAL and NSW community demands a level of skill, commitment, and discipline that are extreme, even within the special operations community. For the very few men who complete the BUD/S program and then make a career as an NSW warrior, the demands and dangers never let up. As long as he is on a SEAL team, life is a continuous cycle of workups and deployments to the sandbox or other exotic travel destinations.

The men of the SBSs, like the crew of this Mk V special operations craft (SOC) lighting up the beach with their M2HB .50-cal machine guns, endure training and missions nearly as dangerous and demanding as their brother warriors on the SEAL teams, but without much of the glory. They do, however, get a full measure of credit from the guys on the teams, especially when they show up to collect a squad from a mission ashore. They are much more than a taxi service for SEALs and execute missions entirely on their own.

(Continued from page 114)

Deployment and Tasking

"Since the time I started in this business twenty-five years ago, I've seen a lot of changes. One is that now our people expect to receive their missions while sitting here in the States or in some forward-deployed base overseas—receipt of mission from higher authority, rather than developing our own missions from within the area where we will operate. In Vietnam we set up our own bases, designed our own missions, and, unless somebody thought we were doing something really stupid, we were left alone. Now we are directed by higher authority. When Ray Smith was operating in the Gulf, he was getting messages from the CINC [commander in chief] saying, 'Conduct SEAL operations here, here, and here.'"

Planning and Accountability

"We've become very good at developing overhead intelligence-collecting from aircraft and satellites. We've lost the ability to develop good human intelligence, the ability to develop information from people, face-to-face. We were great at that, and it was so much better than what we even get now from the overhead systems. But you only get human intelligence by living there, by being part of the community, by building rapport with the host nation—it's the only way that will work. Now we do our planning in an insular way.

"Now I receive my intel, develop a concept or a series of options for an operation, and then I have to send it back to my boss and say, 'Here's what I intend to do; what do you think?' He may have to run the idea up the chain of command even further! Then he'll come back and say, 'This is the one I choose for you.' Then I have to develop that option—and send it up to my boss for approval again! It comes back with his changes . . . and only then can you brief your people. All this time the platoon is milling around, trying to get organized for something—but they aren't at all sure just what it will be.

"This kind of micro-management is the sort of thing we were getting into down in Panama. We were getting into operations where we required outside people, who weren't on the ground

This page and opposite: SEALs have been putting a lot of lead downrange lately, sometimes very far from the beach. In the process, they've been out on the pointy end of the spear, accomplishing missions for the Global War on Terrorism all out of proportion to the number of guns they have in the fight. Individual SEALs have been awarded two Navy Crosses, twenty-three Silver Stars, eight Legions of Merit, and more than five hundred Bronze Stars with V device for valor. Forty-eight Purple Hearts have been awarded (at this writing) for SEALs wounded and killed in action.

with us, telling us how we were going to do things, based on our written plan—asking for permission, which is asking for trouble.

"We tend to do more of our planning now for somebody else, rather than for the teams, to demonstrate that we know how to do something when we're evaluated by our higher authority, or in an exercise where we're demonstrating to an umpire that we're doing things according to doctrine. If you were to take that same platoon and turn them out into an op area for six months where they eat, breathe, and live in the area, like we did on the barges in the Persian Gulf during the Iran-Iraq war, pretty soon you fall into the old habits. You know your operation on the basis of the lowest common denominator and use the KISS principle [keep it simple, stupid!]. That way you have fewer things go wrong, you have a simpler operation to run, you rely on your knowledge of your platoon to deal with contingencies. That's called *flexibility*."

SEAL Virtues and Vices

"We're quite good at maritime direct action missions—where we ourselves are out there, in the water, delivering the munitions, collecting reconnaissance. Second, we are capable of doing long-range, long-duration missions, but we haven't typically been very good at it. The reason is that when you do these long missions, with all their logistics support requirements, you lose the ability to be fast, light, mobile. The minute you start putting on hundred-pound packs you lose that ability to do what we've traditionally done best."

Training Environment vs. the Real World

"I see a lot of guys who just don't get serious about our business. People have a tendency in training, in noncombat exercises, to take shortcuts. We can't afford to do that in this business. The way that you train is the way that you fight. If you get used to taking shortcuts because it's not dangerous, you'll get killed by that shortcut out in the real world. The business that we do is inherently dangerous anyway—parachuting, diving with closed-circuit rigs, locking out of submarines, working with explosives, shooting close to each other—those things are dangerous, but there is a difference even between doing them in training and in combat.

"I cannot explain to somebody until they see it for themselves what it is like to have somebody fall down beside them with a bullet in them, blood coming out of them—to lose a friend—to explain to them that they are vulnerable. You feel like you are almost invincible until you see something like that—and you never get that same feeling in any exercise, no matter how tough we make it. It takes something like that to make you really get serious about this business.

"Because there aren't real bullets going by overhead, people today don't realize you don't go very far very fast in combat. We have a tendency today to say we can travel twelve nautical miles an hour—a figure that is only realistic in a noncombat environment. It was not unusual in Vietnam to take an hour to go a hundred meters back then; you had noise control, mud to contend with, water up to your chest. A hundred meters in an hour was rather fast. But we typically expect much faster movement from our SEALs today.

"Another thing we need to learn is to stop carrying all this extra gear; lighter, faster, smaller is better! I see guys going out with two hundred rounds—you don't need all that. You need to stay mobile, you need to stay light, you don't want to sink too deep in the mud. You need to go back to basics again . . . when you get in the real world.

"But when I left SEAL Team Three we had only five guys out of two hundred and five people who ever had any combat time—and I'll bet that, out of those five guys, not all of them had ever seen anybody get hurt! So you've got five guys who are serious and about two hundred who say, 'I like this job, it's neat, it's fun . . .' Years ago, when we had teams come back with ten of the fourteen guys on a platoon having been wounded, we had a lot of guys who said ' . . . Uh, look, I don't want to do this anymore, I think I'll get out.' We don't have that now because we don't have all those casualties."

Technology—A Blessing and a Curse

"Our weapons system, operating gear, and radios are all better now than ever before. Technology has helped us in many ways, but now we tend to load up on this stuff, because we have it. I've actually stopped people getting ready for an operation and had them weigh their packs—which turned out to weigh a hundred and ten pounds—for a three-day operation, and I say, 'What's wrong with this picture?' You don't need to do that!

You need a couple of LRRPs [similar to MREs], enough water to get you by for that period, your weapon and ammunition—and that's it. Let's go! Batteries, maybe an extra radio, no more than that.

"We have a tendency today to do more whiz-bang stuff, night vision sight systems, laser aim-point systems; it's smaller/lighter/faster today. If I had to go back over there today, I think we'd operate pretty much the same kind of ops."

Joint Operations and the Multi-Service Environment

"In Vietnam, our boat support units lived with us in the same hut. I could go over to the next bunk and say, 'We're going on an op tomorrow night. Can you have this boat ready to go?' Nowadays assets like boats are coordinated by multi-services. If I need a boat now, even though it's internal, I have to make sure everybody knows about it because somebody else may be planning to use the same boat. So, I have to go to higher authority, tell them I need this boat, get my ticket punched, then I can go over to the guy on the next bunk and talk to him about it. If it's a helicopter that could belong to the air force or the army, I might have to go all the way up the chain of command, find out if it's okay, involve them in my planning process, make them part of the mission planning. Since I'm not living in my op area, I have to rely on higher head-quarters to de-conflict my mission, to make sure that they aren't sending an army Green Beret A team into the same area, where we might end up shooting at each other.

"We used to be well-segregated from other friendly units in Vietnam. We all had our assigned AO [Area of Operations], and you didn't cross over without checking with the other team. The same thing applied to the boat units—I could go to the riverine boat commander and say, 'You guys working in here? No? Well, we are, and I don't want you going in there with your boats now.' Nowadays you can't do it that simple."

Parachute Operations for SEALs

"The rule for parachute operations is: If you have to jump, go find another way; if you still can't find another way, make sure you observe the restrictions on wind speed, weights, all that. We have a tendency to make things more complicated than they need to be—we should always go to the lowest common denominator. We have a tendency to send more people than we need when instead we ought to take the minimum. That makes for much better command and control."

Chapter 8

SEALs AT WAR—
CHANGE OF MISSION FOR NSW

SEAL team leader with Special Operations Task Force–South guides Afghan commandos on a foot patrol during an operation to impede insurgent activity in the Khakrez district in the Kandahar province, Afghanistan, 12 March 2011. The commandos are with the 3rd Commando Kandak. *U.S. Army photo by Spc. Daniel P. Shook*

Since the attack on 9/11, there have been a lot of changes in the way American special operations forces are used. In the past, the army's Special Forces, Rangers, and Delta all competed with the navy's SEALs and Special Boat Teams for special operations money, missions, and "trigger time." The air force also had its own special operators on the ground, and the marines did too. Today, however, there is an amazing amount of cooperation and mutual support. For example, you can find U.S. Air Force personnel integrated into SEAL missions, parachuting with them, hiking with them, and fighting alongside the SEALs.

SEAL snipers have been extremely active during many combat operations in Iraq and Afghanistan, supporting conventional forces of the Army such as the 4th Infantry Division. By military doctrine, using SEALs for operations far from water does not seem to make sense. But today, SEALs are a resource for combat commanders and have been used a lot.

SEAL snipers rank with the best combat marksmen in the world. Shown here is a SEAL sniper in a gilly suit, photographed during a capabilities demonstration at Joint Expeditionary Base Little Creek, Virginia. *U.S. Navy photo by Chief Mass Communication Specialist Stan Travioli*

Trigger Time

Before 2003, when American units began sustained ground combat operations in Afghanistan, SEALs trained for war but seldom actually engaged in combat. Since 2003, NAVSPECWARCOM has been making sure that SEALs are all being "blooded." SEALs are now rotated in and out of Afghanistan and Iraq, and the team guys make kills. It is not a pretty subject, and the WARCOM public affairs office will not talk about it, but killing enemy combatants has become a high training priority for every member of a SEAL team. Range time is one thing; putting bullets into people is different. It is an activity that BUD/S cannot simulate.

While most American military personnel deploy for twelve months or more, SEAL teams typically spend only one hundred days "downrange." The operations tempo is higher, SEALs get beat up by the missions, and they rotate back to CONUS after a little more than three months. This "churning" would be a problem for conventional units, but it has worked for the SEALs. And it also makes sure that everybody gets "trigger time."

Unconventional Warfare

NAVSPECWARCOM now claims "unconventional warfare" (UW) as one of the missions for the SEAL/SBS community. U.S. Army Special Forces, or Green Berets, find this claim hilarious. The Green Berets have been experts in UW for more than fifty years; it is the foundation of their mission. They are legendary for missions involving covert insertion of teams (the

A U.S. Navy SEAL team member with Special Operations Task Force–South provides security during a clearing operation in the Panjwai district of Kandahar province, Afghanistan, in April 2011. *U.S. Army photo by Spc. Daniel P. Shook*

SEALs in Kuwait operate Desert Patrol Vehicles (DPV) while preparing for an upcoming February 2002 mission. Each "dune buggy" is outfitted with complex communication and weapon systems designed for the harsh desert terrain. The SEALs' use of the dune buggy DPVs harkens back to the legendary David Stirling's Special Air Service of World War II fame and their "taxi service" in North Africa, the Long Range Desert Group. *U.S. Navy photo by Photographer's Mate 1st Class Arlo Abrahamson*

legendary A-team or A-detachment, as it is known today, is designed around the UW mission) behind enemy lines for long periods.

As developed by the Green Berets, a UW mission requires foreign language skills, the ability to fit into a foreign culture, and the ability to recruit, train, equip, and lead a battalion-sized force of fighters as was done in World War II by OSS teams in France, Italy, and Indochina. Green Berets have all these skills. They train for them in their Q Course and test them in deployments around the world—it's their primary business. SEALs do many things exceptionally well, but foreign language skills and cultural sensitivity are not part of their program. When SEALs interact with foreign nationals, it is often by killing them. Traditional UW is the Green Beret's business. When NAVSPECWARCOM claims a UW mission for the SEALs, it seems like JSOC politics.

The Myth of the Best Warrior

When SEALs make the news, reporters frequently make foolish remarks about them being "the best warriors in the world." This silly comment is not true and would be a risky thing to say in the company of, for example, members of Delta. There is no way to measure the overall quality of groups of combatants, and there are many kinds of "best" to consider.

The British Special Air Service (SAS) and Special Boat Service have both proved superb at many kinds of special operations. The British have a selection and training program that is exquisitely difficult for any special operations force (SOF) team member. The Russian Spetznaz have their own amazing skill set. The U.S. Army's Rangers also have their own brand of "best," with skills and training different from SEALs. And the army's Special Forces, along with the spin-off Delta Force, conduct missions that SEALs would find outside their training and doctrine, particularly the behind-the-lines, long-term guerilla missions called "unconventional warfare."

Each of these communities exists for a specific kind of mission, and each is trained, equipped, and plans for different problems. As one Green Beret battalion commander told me, "We're all pretty much cross-trained on each other's missions, and all of us are trained to conduct raids, water operations, deep reconnaissance, and some kinds of unconventional warfare. Within the American special operations community, SEALs are

Navy SEALs from all over the country took turns pounding the Tridents taken from their uniforms into the casket of Special Warfare Operator (SEAL) 3rd Class Denis Miranda during his 30 September 2010 funeral. One U.S. Army Special Forces operator placed his SF patch on the casket. Miranda was one of nine military service members killed when the helicopter in which they were traveling crashed in Zabul Province in Southern Afghanistan. *U.S. Navy photo by Mass Communication Specialist 2nd Class John Scorza*

the best at maritime operations, but you can't say they are the best at everything."

SEALs are "best" worldwide, as far as we can tell, at missions involving maritime environments—operations with "one foot in the water," as they say. They are also superb at small-unit raids and small direct-action missions, but perhaps no better than Rangers, Recon, Delta, or some army Special Forces units. And the British SAS operators are probably the equal of them all.

But SEALs as well as the rest of these SOF warriors would fail miserably if tasked with the kind of "unconventional warfare" mission that's been the foundation of the Green Berets since

their "birth" in the early 1950s—a mission that requires foreign language skills, tact, diplomacy, and an ability to operate behind enemy lines for months at a time. Tact and diplomacy are not taught at BUD/S, but they are a big part of the Q Course for Green Berets. SEALs are the best at beach surveys, and Green Berets are best at long-term behind-the-lines missions—and there's no yardstick that can measure one skill against the other.

Master-at-Arms 2nd Class (SEAL) Michael A. Monsoor poses for a photo during Operation Iraqi Freedom. Monsoor was posthumously awarded the Medal of Honor for diving onto a grenade to save his teammates in Ar Ramadi, Iraq on 29 September 2006. Monsoor also received the Silver Star for his actions in May during the same deployment in 2006 when he exposed himself to heavy enemy fire to rescue and treat an injured teammate. *U.S. Navy photo courtesy Monsoor family*

Navy SEAL Lt. Michael P. Murphy was posthumously awarded the Medal of Honor for his actions on 28 June 2005 while leading a four-man team tasked with finding a key Taliban leader in the mountains near Asadabad, Afghanistan. The team came under fire from a much larger enemy force with superior tactical position. Murphy left his cover to get a clear radio signal with his headquarters and was mortally wounded while exposing himself to enemy fire. Murphy provided his unit's location and requested immediate support. He returned to his cover position to continue the fight until finally succumbing to his wounds. *U.S. Navy photo*

Lessons Learned

If the Naval Special Warfare community has learned anything, it is that even SEALs are not bulletproof. The sailor who gets through BUD/S and proves himself on a team is an exceptionally capable warrior who rightfully owns a big ego. Unsurprisingly, they used to have a tendency to feel a bit bulletproof.

The bulletproof mentality went away after Petty Officer Neil Roberts was killed in Afghanistan in 2002. Then Lt. Michael Murphy, Petty Officer Matthew Axelson, and Petty Officer Danny Dietz were all killed in a combat operation on 28 June 2005. Eight other SEALs coming to their rescue were also killed, along with eight U.S. Army Night Stalkers helicopter crewmen. It was the deadliest day in SEAL history up to that point. Marc Lee was killed in combat on 2 August 2006, the first SEAL killed in Iraq.

SEALs make mistakes—sometimes lethal mistakes, even in training—that may be a result of the bulletproof attitude. While working on the first edition of this book, one of the SEALs I was photographing had a "negligent discharge" of his M4 carbine and shot a teammate two or three times at very close range. The same week, another platoon from the same team had a vehicle rollover, resulting in several fatalities. Neither made news because NSW public affairs did not release information.

The last ten years of combat operations have been good for NSW. Training standards remain high, budgets are generous, and plenty of excellent young sailors still apply for BUD/S. Selection and training processes have been refined so that BUD/S and SEAL Qualification and Training (SQT) produces guys who are better prepared than ever.

As a result of lessons learned, deployments are also done differently. Now the teams deploy as complete units. Everybody goes downrange together—the commander, the staff, the supply section, and the support units. Teams are now more sensitive to issues and able to respond quickly.

"At My Command . . . FIRE!"— The Counter-Piracy Mission

The U.S. Navy, Marine Corps, and Coast Guard have been

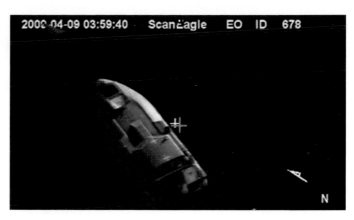

A 28-foot lifeboat from the U.S.-flagged container ship *Maersk Alabama* is shown in this still frame from a video taken by a ScanEagle unmanned aerial vehicle flying over the Indian Ocean, 9 April 2009. *U.S. Navy*

A ScanEagle unmanned aerial vehicle launches from the flight deck aboard amphibious dock landing ship USS *Comstock* (LSD 45) in the Persian Gulf, 20 May 2011. ScanEagle carries an electro-optical and/or infrared camera, has a communications range over 100 kilometers, and can fly 20-plus hours. ScanEagle has a 10-foot wingspan and has an average cruising speed of 60 knots. *Mass Communication Specialist 2nd Class Joseph M. Buliavac, U.S. Navy*

A team from the amphibious assault ship USS *Boxer* (LHD 4) tows the lifeboat from the *Maersk Alabama* to the *Boxer* 13 April 2009 in the Indian Ocean. The lifeboat is to be processed for evidence after the successful rescue of Capt. Richard Phillips. *Mass Communication Specialist 2nd Class Jon Rasmussen, U. S. Navy*

conducting anti-piracy missions on the high seas for years, normally without much fanfare or media coverage. Hundreds of ships are attacked by pirates every year, sometimes with violence, often at great expense to their owners. Despite the threat and its associated costs, piracy in the Gulf of Aden did not get much attention until early April 2009. Four Somali pirates boarded the freighter *Maersk Alabama* and took the captain, Richard Phillips, hostage.

This was the first capture of an American-flagged merchant ship in two hundred years, and it provoked two major changes by the American government, both involving SEALs. Prior to this event, pirates usually ransomed the vessels for large amounts of money, normally without bloodshed. But since the capture of the *Alabama*, merchant ships now resist capture, and there is plenty of bloodshed.

In response to this capture on 8 April 2009, the U.S. Navy sent the USS *Bainbridge* to the scene. The destroyer arrived the next day, 9 April. After attempting to exchange a captured pirate for Captain Phillips, the other pirates backed out, taking Phillips hostage in one of the *Alabama*'s lifeboats.

In previous circumstances, ransom was paid. But now the navy was confrontational and ordered two other ships to the scene, the amphibious assault ship USS *Boxer* and frigate USS *Halliburton*. The *Bainbridge* began blocking the pirate's lifeboat from returning to shore. After two days of negotiation and

MV *Maersk Alabama* Capt. Richard Phillips thanks U.S. sailors on board USS *Bainbridge* (DDG 96) in Port Norfolk, Virginia, 19 November 2009, for their part in his rescue from Somali pirates. *Mass Communication Specialist 3rd Class David Danals, Department of Defense*

A sniper fires an SR-25 rifle from a helicopter. The weapon is supported by a vibration-isolating web of bungee cords that dampen the motion of the aircraft. It's not the most stable platform for a sniper, but it's the best option under the circumstances. *U.S. Navy*

threats, the on-scene commander, Commander Frank Costellano, determined that Phillip's life was in danger. Costellano authorized the use of force against the three pirates.

During the night of 10 April, several SEAL snipers with weapons and gear parachuted into the sea. They were picked up and delivered covertly to *Bainbridge*. Three of the group were snipers from SEAL Team Six (ST6). After being briefed

and establishing secure comms with the destroyer's CIC (combat information center), the three snipers took up firing positions on the *Bainbridge*'s stern and began preparing to engage the three pirates.

Five days after Phillips was taken hostage, the lifeboat was getting low on fuel, and the pirates appeared to be becoming extremely stressed. The pirates agreed to take a tow from the

Visit, board, search, and seizure (VBSS) team members from the guided-missile cruiser USS *Vella Gulf* (CG 72) close in on rigid-hulled inflatable boats on 12 February 2009 to apprehend suspected pirates. Nine suspected pirates were apprehended and brought aboard. *Vella Gulf* is the flagship for Combined Task Force 151, a multinational task force conducting counter-piracy operations to detect and deter piracy in and around the Gulf of Aden, Arabian Gulf, Indian Ocean, and Red Sea. *Mass Communications Specialist 2nd Class Jason R. Zalasky, U.S. Navy*

SEAL snipers provide overwatch security during VBSS missions and are able to detect and engage threats not visible to the boarding team. The small dots visible in the rifle's reticule allow a trained sniper to estimate range with enough precision to deliver accurate fire at long ranges. Even so, maritime sniper engagements are among the most difficult and challenging for SEALs and other snipers, since both the target and the weapon are in constant motion. *Author's collection*

normal for the optics normally mounted on sniper rifles. Second, the targets were moving about the boat. And one of the pirates was behind one of the Plexiglas windows of the lifeboat, a material that would probably deflect a bullet.

With one of the pirates always holding an AK on Captain Phillips, the possibility that the hostage would die in any use of force was high. The team developed a plan to engage all three pirates with simultaneous shots. The chance came when two pirates peered from open hatches while the third was visible through a window. Communicating by radio, all three snipers fired at the same moment, each at a pre-designated target. Two apparently used .308-caliber SR-25s, the third a heavier .338 Lapuaa Magnum or possibly even a .50 caliber. All three pirates were killed instantly by head shots.

The legacy of this engagement has been profound. Piracy off the horn of Africa and in the western Pacific is taken far more seriously now than before the *Maersk Alabama* mission. Today, largely overlooked by the media, there is an active counter-piracy campaign operating. Snipers from American special operations forces (SOF) and those of other nations are stationed aboard ships transiting the Gulf of Aden and other trouble spots. Some are active-duty snipers from teams with special assignment missions; some are contractors working directly for shipping companies. Either way, they are typically armed with sniper rifles in heavy calibers (.300 WinMag, .338 Lapuua, .50 caliber). They carry NODs, good comm gear, and are "armed" with the authority to "discourage" piracy on the high seas.

ship and attached a line to the lifeboat. This stabilized the lifeboat and put it much closer to the SEALs' firing position.

The SEAL snipers had several serious challenges. The range from their position on the *Bainbridge*'s fantail to their targets was extremely short, about 40 meters. That is much closer than

Chapter 9

AMERICA'S MOST WANTED—
THE MISSION TO KILL OSAMA BIN LADEN

At approximately 2330 hours local time, 1 May 2011, a small armada of helicopters pulled pitch and lifted off on a mission that had been planned and practiced for weeks. Watching closely from the other side of the world, the president and the National Command Authority monitored the mission in real time.

The mission to capture or kill Osama bin Laden, the OBL raid, was a perfect example of what battle staffs call "high risk, high payoff" operations. Beginning nine months earlier, pieces of an enormous puzzle were gradually fitting together, bits of information from thousands of anonymous "intel" specialists from the Central Intelligence Agency (CIA) and elsewhere. As the bits came together, a mission to get Osama bin Laden started to evolve, a mission designed by hundreds of people within Joint Special Operations Command (JSOC).

Afterwards, U.S. Navy SEALS got the credit from the news media, but the mission involved many players from dozens of military communities and special operations forces. For example, the helicopters were from the army's Night Stalkers, the 160th Special Operations Aviation Regiment (SOAR), a unit that is even more covert than the SEAL teams. The Night Stalkers have been practicing and perfecting nighttime air assault missions for many years.

The first two MH-60 Black Hawk helicopters leading the mission held about twenty-two assault team members, mostly U.S. Navy SEALs, but including some agents of the CIA, one combat dog and handler, and an interpreter. The two MH-60s delivering the assault teams were both modified versions with stealthy characteristics. It's said they do not show up on radar and are, according to reports from operators who have seen them in action, incredibly quiet.

During a Sensitive Site Exploitation mission in the Zhawar Kili area of Eastern Afghanistan on 12 January 2002, members of a U.S. Navy Seal team found valuable intelligence information, including this Osama bin Laden propaganda poster. *Department of Defense*

News reports after the mission will describe only two helicopters on the OBL raid, an impossible number to knowledgeable observers. There were, in fact, probably more than

The new special operations MH-60M Black Hawk brings many impressive capabilities, including state-of-the-art day and night optics systems, enhanced integrated weapons systems, multi-mode radar with all-weather capability, and new high-performance engines. This Blackhawk is the first M model Blackhawk to be received by the army's 160th Special Operations Aviation Regiment. *160th Special Operations Aviation Regiment*

six helicopters plus support aircraft overhead. Two MH-60s can lift only about ten to twelve combat-equipped SEALs, even with the seats out and all combatants sitting on the aircraft floor. Most likely, two MH-60s probably delivered the assault teams, in two groups of eleven, into the compound, while other helicopters delivered the support SEALs to blocking positions nearby.

Besides the assault force, at least one MH-60 was designated as a spare. And for additional insurance, at least one or two additional helicopters, likely including an MH-47 Chinook, carried a security team. Their mission was to protect the objective from any Pakistani response and augment the raiders in the event that the assault team needed backup to deal with enemy defenders inside the compound.

The Art of the Raid

A raid like the one on the bin Laden compound is essentially a "deep strike" mission behind enemy lines. American warfighters have been conducting these missions for over forty years, and it has become a military art form for SEALs, Green Berets, Delta, Rangers, and others. Here are the fundamentals:

"High-risk, high-payoff" operations get extensive planning, beginning with collecting and refining huge amounts of "intel" data. The bin Laden mission started with scraps of information about a courier's identity. The courier was then found and tracked at a distance. When his location was identified, about nine months before the assault, huge

working for the CIA or others rented or purchased homes nearby, within sight of the compound.

Preceding the mission, someone would keep eyes on the place. There would be monitoring, recording, and reporting on all activity, twenty-four hours a day. Surveillance missions are notoriously difficult and dangerous when human eyeballs are required. Today, however, home security systems are so common, even in Pakistan, that cameras pointed at the compound would have caused no comment with the locals. A home security system, purchased in Pakistan and connected to the Internet, could provide a constant feed of information to the intel specialists planning the raid.

Considering the value of the target, the openness of the location, and the amount of time spent on planning the operation, it is very likely that an intense surveillance program was in place for months before the raid. Besides safe houses and overwatch positions, teams would have monitored all activity around the area and driven past the compound on an irregular basis. Listening devices were probably installed. Drone over-flights collected daylight and infrared imagery, as well as cell phone traffic and any other digital information that would be useful.

The E&E Plan

A standard component of the planning for every SEAL and SOF mission is to anticipate what to do when the whole

numbers of overhead photographs of the compound were made. At the same time, covert operators infiltrated the area. Surveillance "safe houses" were set up, and the walled compound was monitored constantly and invisibly.

Safe Houses and Overwatch Surveillance

Early in the planning sequence, soon after the compound was identified, at least one and perhaps three or more surveillance teams went to work. American personnel might have been part of these teams; the Green Berets have the cultural and language skills to infiltrate the area and to covertly watch the compound. But it is more likely that Pakistani nationals mission goes to hell, as it sometimes does. All the SEALs and other raiders on any mission have been briefed on an E&E, or escape-and-evasion plan. Each man has an E&E kit somewhere in his gear, probably in a pants pocket. Every mission briefing includes a detailed discussion of how to escape capture and move back to American forces. For the OBL raid, this would have included the locations of the "safe houses" (a "war RV" in SEAL slang) near the objective, how to find it, how to gain entry, and what support would be available there.

2400 Hours—Launching the Mission

Covert insertions of raid teams follow a standard format, with variations based on the specific tactical situation. For the OBL raid, here is how it probably went down:

The SEALs and other personnel load into at least three and probably more MH-60 helicopters, with about ten SEALs to each aircraft. Two of the MH-60s carry the actual entry teams; another two carry a security element to guard the objective while the raid is conducted.

The SEALs are equipped for only a short time on the ground. They will wear regular body armor and helmets. Most will carry M4 carbines with suppressors and laser aiming systems.

The helicopter crews have flown this mission profile hundreds of times and are entirely comfortable with most of it. After the flight lifts off from its austere launch site in eastern Afghanistan, the aircraft navigation lights are turned off. The pilots use binocular night observation devices (NODs) to watch the terrain below.

Flying "contour" at night under NODs is hugely exciting and very strange, a bit like driving 100 miles per hour on a freeway with no lights. The pilots skim above the ground at 120 knots or more, following the rise and fall of the terrain below. This

Real-time intelligence from American unmanned aerial vehicles (UAVs) is a critical aspect of successfully planning and executing a raid such as the OBL mission. Pictured here, a U.S. Air Force MQ-1B Predator unmanned aerial vehicle takes off. The Predator is 27 feet long with a wingspan of 48.7 feet. It cruises at 70 to 90 knots and has a service ceiling of 25,000 feet. The Predator can fly for 24 hours at a time and has a range of 2,000 nautical miles. Note the AGM-114 Hellfire missiles carried under each wing. The Hellfire is a 100-pound air-to-surface missile that has been in use since the 1980s. *Tech Sergeant Sabrina Johnson, Department of Defense*

133

Crews of the 160th Special Operations Aviation Regiment train extensively for night operations, more than earning the nickname "Night Stalkers." Here, a Night Stalker MH-47 Chinook helicopter pilot adjusts his night vision goggles prior to a night mission during training exercise.

Tech Sergeant Marvin Krause, Department of Defense

technique masks the sound and appearance of the aircraft to observers on the ground, minimizing the risk from ground fire. If you are wearing NODs, the sensation of speed is amazing.

0130 Hours

The two assault helicopters arrive at the compound in trail formation, one behind the other. Standard procedure for such assaults is for one team to take the objective from the roof, the other from the ground, each moving like a methodical snake toward a link-up in the middle.

The OBL raid compound presents some challenges for the Night Stalker crews. There is room inside the walls for one helicopter to land, but it is tight: the rotor arc for the MH-60 is about 53 feet and the compound was about 80 feet across. About 40 yards from the western edge of the compound is a high-tension power line with heavy wires blocking movement from that side. Open fields on either

side, however, offer excellent and unobstructed landing zones for the back-up helicopters.

Two entry teams, each to insert by 160th SOAR MH-60 helicopters with "stealth" modifications, are to assault and clear the compound from two directions. One group of about ten SEALs will be "fast-roping" onto the roof; the other group unloads from an MH-60 landing inside the compound. Each methodically clears its area until the whole compound is secured.

As sometimes happens on such risky missions, a serious problem develops almost immediately. One of the MH-60s attempts to land inside the compound, but loses power and lands hard, sustaining considerable damage. The SEALs aboard move off to execute their mission while the two pilots and two gunners go to work removing weapons and comm gear, then finish up by rigging explosive charges to destroy the damaged aircraft.

A SEAL delivery vehicle team (SDV) fast-ropes to the topside of the *Los Angeles*–class fast attack submarine USS *Toledo* (SSN 769) in 2005; sometimes fast-roping is the only practical way to come aboard. *Journalist 3rd Class Davis J. Anderson, U.S. Navy*

On the OBL mission, SEALs fast-roped onto the roof of the bin Laden compound. All special operations forces practice fast-roping extensively. *Mass Communication Speacialist 2nd Class Sarah E. Bitter*

Fast-roping is often the fastest way to get a team from a helicopter to the objective. SEALs are no exception. *Photographer's Mate 2nd Class Michael J. Pusnik Jr., U.S. Navy*

Breaching one entry point after another, the team clears the ground level and works toward the upper floors where they expect to find their target. Within a few minutes of arrival, they find Osama bin Laden. One of his wives blocks the door, and she is shot in the leg. When bin Laden moves toward the entry team, the SEAL on point places his PEQ-15 laser dot on bin Laden's head and fires, killing him instantly.

The SEAL team then quickly scoops up all the computer hard drives and memory devices, loading them on one of the helicopters. The inert body of bin Laden is also placed on one of the aircraft. While the assault is going down, the crew of the damaged helicopter prepares it for demolition with explosives, then detonates the charges.

At about 0210 hours local time, the SEAL assault teams and support personnel moved to their helicopters and were extracted. The valuables include a treasure-trove of computer memory and a cooling corpse. Sometime around 0300 hours Monday morning local time, the raiders crossed the border and were out of Pakistan. It was Sunday night in the United States when television stations began interrupting programming with the announcement. Spontaneous celebrations result. SEAL Team 6, along with the CIA, the Night Stalkers, and many anonymous people in the counter-terrorism business, had finally slain the architect of the 9/11 attack on America.

Aftermath

In the weeks after the raid, it became clear that killing bin Laden changed a lot of the dynamics of the business of American counter-terror operations. For one thing, the skeptics who predicted that bin Laden would never be found and that the United States would give up and go home were proved wrong by the cooperative efforts of people from many agencies working together with a single goal. For another, the role of Pakistan as a dubious ally was clearly revealed when anybody suspected of supporting the raid—the owners of local safe houses, particularly—were arrested. Since the raid, terrorists worldwide must have the uncomfortable feeling that there is no safe harbor for them anywhere and that any of them can be hunted down and shot in the head, in their own bedroom, in the middle of the night, in the middle of a country that seems otherwise supportive of terrorist organizations.

For Americans, justice was all the sweeter for the long wait.

About the same time, the other half of the SEAL team arrives in an MH-47 Chinook or two more Black Hawks, also flown by Night Stalkers. Landing in a field next to the compound, these SEALs quickly establish a perimeter defense and set up blocking positions on the nearby roads.

In the darkness, the assault teams methodically clear the compound, breaching gates and doors with explosives, moving snakelike through each area. When people are encountered in the compound, each is secured: head shots for men with weapons, flex-cuffs for women and children.

Soldiers with the 10th Special Forces Group ride in a Night Stalker CH-47 Chinook helicopter in March 2011. This is what the inside of the Chinook carrying SEALs and other mission personnel on the bin Laden mission looked like as the raid's helicopters sped through the night air over Pakistan to the bin Laden compound.

Tech Sergeant Manuel J. Martinez, U.S. Air Force

Tactics, Techniques, and Procedures of the Osama bin Laden Raid—Remotely Piloted Vehicles (RPVs) and More

Any observer of American special operations knows that a deliberate raid, one with time for planning and coordination, with the opposing force nearby and all systems available, would include RPVs. Some would provide video coverage and relay radio comms, while other RPVs observe critical locations on the battlefield. There are reports that SOCOM and JSOC have been amused about speculation that drones were used to provide security against Pakistani reaction forces and for other critical elements of the mission. This speculation is silly, because American special ops forces have been doing covert missions for fifty years. The basic planning methods are well known, the resources and the TTPs (tactics, techniques, and procedures) have been public knowledge for many years. Anyone interested

in covert operations knows the capabilities of the drones, about our electronic warfare aircraft, and the use of covert data collection by operatives on the ground. These resources have been part of mission-planning doctrine for decades. So if you discover that Osama bin Laden is living quietly in a little town in Pakistan and his capture is your objective, the business pretty much falls into place.

SPECWARCOM and JSOC are holding back details of the raid. But based on standard SOF mission-planning TTPs and informed commentary from special operations insiders, here are some likely scenarios. SEAL Team 6 was selected for the mission early in the planning sequence. One reason was that they had just returned after a hundred-day deployment to Afghanistan and were in an "operator" mindset still fresh from combat operations. Another was that both SOCOM and JSOC commanders, Admiral Eric Olson

When clearing an objective such as the bin Laden compound, SEALs will move snakelike in a conga line to maintain contact with each other, particularly when in the dark using night observation devices. *U.S. Marine Corps*

and Vice Admiral William McRaven, were former SEALs, former commanders of ST6, and completely confident in ST6 capabilities.

Security for the Isolation Phase of the Mission

While many media reports state that the SEALs conducted their preparations and rehearsals in Afghanistan, the story from inside the SOF community is a more radical but more reasonable scenario. Afghanistan is not secure for the rehearsals needed for a major raid. According to one retired operator, ST6 went into isolation on a military installation in the United States, built a detailed mockup of the compound, and then rehearsed the takedown in our own western desert—someplace in the Southwest. This makes perfect sense. Rehearsals would be conducted with far better security here than elsewhere. Even so, security was so tight that even the command group of ST6 was not briefed on the

details. They reportedly learned the specifics only after the raid had been executed.

Going into Isolation

Missions developed by American SOF units have many standardized procedures. Part of the planning is done by the really quiet members of the community, the staff intelligence specialists and planners. They will collect all information about the target—prisoner interrogation reports, "overhead" imagery from satellites, intercepts from aircraft, drones, radio and telephone, and ground surveillance both overt and covert. People looking like Pakistanis surely drove past the compound, taking photographs. People, also Pakistanis, surely bought or rented homes near the compound and set up surveillance systems to monitor the place around the clock. The intel specialists began quietly collecting every shred of data about the suspected location of OBL.

138

A U.S. Air Force MQ-1 Predator aircraft assigned to the 11th Reconnaissance Squadron, 432nd Air Expeditionary Wing, in flight over the desert. *Master Sgt. Scott Reed, U.S. Air Force*

U.S. Navy Aviation Boatswain's Mate Lowel A. Shorey III directs a U.S. Army CH-47G Chinook helicopter attached to the Night Stalkers of the 160th Special Operations Aviation Squadron performing deck landing qualifications aboard the amphibious transport dock ship USS *Juneau* (LPD 10) while under way on 4 February 2008. *Mass Communication Specialist 1st Class Michael D. Kennedy, U.S. Navy*

When the commander and the planning staff are confident, a team is selected, notified, and transported to an isolation compound. After a team goes into isolation, there is absolutely no contact from friends or family until the mission is executed or cancelled. The SEALs who conducted this mission disappeared for what was probably a month.

Writing the Plan

Any plan begins with a massive collection of intelligence data of all types. The plan will be written by the team who will execute it, with support from the intel weenies, the commanders, and specialists. The team presents their plan to the commander in a "brief back." If the commander gives the plan a "go," something as risky as the OBL raid, with all its political consequences, will go up the chain of command to the NCA (National Command Authority) and ultimately to the guy called POTUS, the president of the United States.

SEALs train extensively using full-scale mockups. Here, SEALs practice room clearing, which was a vital part of the bin Laden mission. *Mass Communication Specialist 2nd Class Eddie Harrison, U.S. Navy*

Helicopters for the bin Laden raid were transported using C-17 Globemaster II cargo aircraft. The C-17 is big enough to carry any helicopters used by the army, including the special ops Black Hawks and Chinooks of the Night Stalkers. Pictured here is a conventional army Chinook being transported inside a C-17. *Staff Sergeant Stacy Fowler, U.S. Air Force*

When approved, details remain secret, but the standard mission procedures are common knowledge. It is standard procedure for the team to go into isolation early. The target will be duplicated as well as possible, the whole operation will be rehearsed endlessly, and potential disasters will be considered.

Launching the Mission

According to rumors, the OBL mission actually launched from the United States. ST6 spent about a full month in isolation, working on the op order and rehearsing the execution. When the mission launched, the whole assault force—about forty SEALs, about twenty helicopter crewmen, at least four and possibly more helicopters, plus CIA folks, and a combat dog—were loaded onto U.S. Air Force C-17s and flown directly to a remote location near Abbottabad where the final phase of the raid would begin.

There is a standard procedure for deliberate raids on high-value targets. When army helicopters from the 160th

SOAR are involved, they are embedded from the outset. So the MH-60s and their crews also went into isolation with ST6. And when the SEALs loaded onto the C-17s, the helicopters and crews were aboard.

One helicopter was probably a MH-47 Chinook with high-lift capacity. A C-17 can carry a Chinook or a Black Hawk plus the helicopter's crew. It can also carry all the SEALs and other raid personnel all on the gear at the same time.

This is just informed speculation, but it makes sense that around 28 April, a series of C-17s departed from a very secure airfield on a military base in the United States with the entire raid package—twenty-two raiders, another twenty or thirty for backup, a security element, a couple of interpreters, a combat dog and handler, helicopters, weapons, and the finest communication gear tax dollars can buy. With relief crews, the C-17s can fly direct from, say, Nellis Air Force Base to eastern Afghanistan in about seventeen hours. The aircraft would meet tankers to refuel three or four times en route.

Highly trained combat dogs, with a sense of smell that is forty times more sensitive than a human's, can provide an important force multiplier to a SEAL team. A combat dog and handler were part of the bin Laden mission. *Chief Mass Communication Specialist Stan Travioli, U.S. Navy*

If security is a critical factor, how can the commander and his staff make their transition from the C-17s to the helicopters without drawing unwanted attention? One way might be to avoid landing at any airfield at all. The C-17 is designed for rough, short, airfields that can be nothing more than a stretch of desert. It is possible to land far from any military facility and also quite possible to land in Pakistan, even closer to the objective. When planning very high risk raids in denied territory, closer is better and is a standard operating procedure.

Once on the ground, the helicopters were unloaded, the blades unfolded and pins replaced, and the crews prepped for flight. The SEALs and others on the team would "kit up," putting on their tactical vests, checking weapons, checking NODs, checking radios. This might have happened in the dark, sometime after 1900 hours or so local time. Team leaders would have inspected their men and all would have been inside their helicopters by 2400.

A Stealthy Insertion

Speculation surrounds the Abbottabad raid. How could you fly helicopters into essentially "denied" territory without being engaged by Pakistani defenses? Do you disguise the helicopters with Pakistani colors? Can you "spoof" the transponder codes used to identify aircraft, mimicking Pakistani military helicopters? Can you be invisible to radar by structural modifications to the helicopter blades and airframe?

The MH-60 helicopters used for the assault each cost about $15 million, three times the cost of a conventional UH-60 Black Hawk. Some of that extra $10 million went into navigation and communications systems, but some also went to modify the rotors. "Those things are deathly quiet," one SOF operator says.

Night Stalker pilots are masters of flying "contour" at night, without lights. This is another way to become invisible to both radar and ground observers. NOE, or "nap of the earth" flight is wonderfully exciting. The sensation of speed at 100 miles per hour and 100 feet above ground is much greater than 1,000 miles per hour at 10,000 feet. Flying NOE is dangerous in daytime and more so at night, but it is the best way to fly behind enemy lines.

Chapter 10

TODAY'S SEALs— IN THEIR OWN WORDS

Since the first Gulf War, threats to global security have changed tremendously. Some of these changes predate the 9/11 attacks, some are independent of them. Regardless of the reasons, all members of American special operations forces are in high demand today. SEALs and other members of the special operations community are busy today in such numbers and in such important roles that operations in Afghanistan have been called the "special operations war." Navy SEALs are cooperating with some previously unlikely forces in operations that were unthinkable a decade or so ago. Not only are SEALs working alongside Green Berets and Rangers, they've developed a close and affectionate partnership with the Polish special forces teams, *Grupa Reagowania Operacyjno Mobilnego* (GROM; operational mobile response group). GROM, established in 1991, has demonstrated great proficiency in conducting small unit direct action missions.

Among the many unsung heroes of SEAL missions today are some very tough and brave navy sailors—the members of the explosive ordnance disposal (EOD) units. They are not SEALs and not part of NSW, but these personnel support many demanding NSW missions. With the prevalence of bombs and booby traps in the current area of operations, the role of the EOD specialists has become essential. Their training is more specialized than that of SEALs, but members of this small community are as physically tough as the SEALs they support. You will find EOD personnel and their specialized gear on vessel boardings, raids, and operations where their skills are needed.

The SEALs also continue to work with the "special boat guys," the special warfare combatant crewmembers (SWCC). The SWCC have for years been conducting maritime interdiction operations in the Persian Gulf area to enforce sanctions imposed during the Gulf War. After 9/11, they conducted operations to prevent al Qaeda and Taliban members from escaping the area in merchant ships and fishing boats. Before the official start of Operation Iraqi Freedom, SEALs and SWCC were key assets employed to secure the southern oil infrastructures of the Al-Faw peninsula and the offshore gas and oil terminals. The ability of the United States to secure these facilities prevented ecological disaster and saved precious financial resources for the people of Iraq. SWCC were also involved in clearing the Khor Al Abdullah and Khor Az Zubayar waterways that enabled the first humanitarian aid to be delivered to the vital port city of Umm Qasr. SWCC and members of the SEAL delivery vehicle teams have also been put to work in the tactical operations centers (TOCs), where the commanders of all special operations forces command and control their forces. Their background in the planning and conduct of special operations missions makes them especially valuable as planners and communicators with SEAL and other teams deployed "downrange."

Buried Treasure at Zhawar Kili

In January 2002, a SEAL team supported by a platoon of marines was inserted by helicopter into the mountainous region of Zhawar Kili, an area in eastern Afghanistan near the border with Pakistan. The mission was a reconnaissance of a location known to support Taliban forces and was scheduled to last twelve hours. Once on the ground, however, the SEALs discovered an immense network of about seventy underground storage facilities stuffed with many tons of

During a Sensitive Site Exploitation (SSE) mission, SEALs explore the entrance to one of seventy caves they discovered in Zhawar Kili area. Used by al Qaeda and Taliban forces, the caves and other above-ground complexes were subsequently destroyed either by navy Explosive Ordnance Disposal (EOD) personnel or through air strikes called in by the SEALs. *U.S. Navy.*

explosives and ammunition. This cave complex had been reinforced with concrete, steel beams, and bricks. The SEALs and marines found classrooms, offices, and cooking and sleeping quarters sufficient for a large force and virtually invisible from the air.

The SEALs and marines were lightly supplied with MREs and water but not equipped for extended operations in the high, cold mountains. They stayed anyway and got to work destroying the enemy supplies. Although they had some blasting materials of their own, there were far too many bunkers to be blown with the available supply.

An abandoned village was found nearby and used as a temporary base. It took two days, but then marine helicopters flew in water, sleeping bags, additional MREs, and

other gear while the demo specialists got to work. The contents of the bunkers was inventoried, then destroyed. Navy aircraft delivered precision-guided bombs with delayed fuses into the mouths of the caves, causing secondary explosions of the enemy munitions which shook the whole valley.

"I Had a Blast"—ABH1 Neil Roberts, Navy SEAL

This is a very busy time for members of the NSW community, a time of intense training and deployments, of new responsibilities and missions. These are largely invisible to the American public by the design of NSW, except when a SEAL or SWCC is killed. Only then is a glimpse inside real world operations possible.

SEALs lay down covering fire as part of an extraction exercise during a July 2010 capabilities demonstration at Joint Expeditionary Base Little Creek, Virginia. *U.S. Navy photo by Chief Mass Communication Specialist Stan Travioli*

ABH1 Neil Roberts died on a mission somewhat typical of NSW operations in this new kind of war. Roberts was a career SEAL, a big, cheerful guy from a big, cheerful family. He loved the navy and especially the SEALs.

In early March 2002, Roberts was aboard one of two army CH-47 Chinook helicopters participating in Operation Anaconda in the Shah-i-Kot valley south of Kabul. This area was a major stronghold for Taliban and al Qaeda forces, and Anaconda was designed to destroy these enemy forces. In the past, SEALs would have been tasked with a small mission away from the main operation, but during Anaconda, Roberts and his team were fighting alongside Rangers and Green Berets, being transported by army helicopter, and cooperating with Afghan Mujahadeen freedom fighters. Intel reports suggested that about 250 enemy personnel were in the area, and that they would try to escape toward nearby Pakistan if pushed.

Major General Frank Hagenbeck, the task force commander, sent his forces into positions at three critical terrain features—battle positions Heather, Ginger, and Eve.

Their landing zone was deep inside Afghanistan, hundreds of miles from any beach, on a hill mass indicated on the maps by the code name "Whale". This site was one of the few suitable places for the insertion of forces by helicopter, and enemy forces accordingly emplaced defenders nearby for just such an assault.

Roberts was standing on the ramp of his Chinook, manning an M249 SAW (squad automatic weapon), a machine gun that fires the same 5.56mm round used by the M16 and M4 carbine. As his helicopter flared before landing, nose high and speed rapidly diminishing, the enemy defenders cut loose with all available weapons, AK-47s and RPGs predominating. The helicopter was hit by numerous rounds, pitched

SEALs discover a cache of munitions and weapons while conducting a sensitive site exploitation (SSE) mission in the Jaji mountains of Afghanistan on 12 February 2002. *U.S. Navy photo by Photographer's Mate 1st Class Tim Turner*

nose up, and thrashed violently as the pilots aborted the landing and struggled out of the kill zone.

At some point during this barrage, the two machine gunners on the ramp were ejected from the aircraft. One, an army crewman, was secured by his gunner's belt to a tie-down on the aircraft floor and was hauled back aboard. Roberts was unsecured and dropped between five and ten feet to the ground without his M249.

In the confusion of the moment, with the Chinook crew struggling for their lives, Roberts would have to wait for attention, but not for long. The dying helicopter crash-landed nearby, and the crew hastily mounted a rescue mission.

An unmanned reconnaissance drone aircraft over the scene transmitted video back to Bagram Airbase and recorded what happened next. Despite the tumble from the helicopter, Roberts kept his wits. He activated his rescue beacon, then crawled to a terrain position offering cover and

U.S. Navy SEALs along with their Afghan partner forces conduct a tactical ground movement during a four-day clearing operation of the lower Char Chineh Valley in Uruzgan province, Afghanistan, in late June 2011. They conducted the joint operation to deny insurgents sanctuary and staging areas in order to secure the surrounding military bases and checkpoints. *U.S. Army photo by Staff Sergeant Kaily Brown*

concealment from the small arms fire directed at him. He fought back with his pistol and grenades. According to reports, he was seen assaulting a machine gun position. He continued to fight for about an hour, killing enemy soldiers with his pistol, sometimes at very close range, one SEAL against an estimated sixty Taliban soldiers.

The drone's video camera apparently saw Roberts hit by enemy fire several times, but he continued to fight. Out of grenades and pistol magazines, Roberts finally collapses and dies.

Any sense of victory felt by the Taliban forces on the Whale were short-lived. The rescue force arrived about two hours later—helicopters loaded with air force para-rescue-

men, Rangers, and SEALs. These helicopters also encountered ground fire but were not taken by surprise. The rescue force was too late to save Roberts, but they were in time to slay the enemy on the ridge. Fighting was, as they say, intense, and few prisoners were taken. Six Americans were killed and many others wounded.

ABH1 Neil Roberts was posthumously awarded the Silver Star, Bronze Star with Valor designation, and the Purple Heart. His wife Patty released parts of a letter he left to be opened in the event of his death. In part, it read:

"Although I sacrificed personal freedom and many other things, I got just as much as I gave. My time in the Teams was special. For all the times I was cold, wet, tired, sore, scared, hungry and angry, I had a blast. All the times spent in the company of my teammates was when I felt the closest to the men I had the privilege to work with. I loved being a SEAL. If I died doing something for the Teams, then I died doing what made me happy. Very few people have the luxury of that."

A Navy SEAL shares an MRE (meal, ready to eat) with local Afghani children on 24 January 2002. The SEALs were in the area during a a sensitive site exploitation (SSE) mission to find suspected al Qaeda and Taliban. *U.S. Navy photo by Photographer's Mate 1st Class Tim Turner*

A SEAL platoon hangs beneath an HH-60H Seahawk helicopter assigned to the "Red Wolves" of Helicopter Sea Combat Squadron 84 during a July 2010 special patrol insertion/extraction (SPIE) demonstration at Joint Expeditionary Base Little Creek–Fort Story, Virginia—*Department of Defense photo by Mass Communication Specialist 2nd Class Matt Daniels.*

Capturing the Taliban

Members of SEAL Team 5 executed over three hundred combat operations during one six-month deployment in 2003, an "op tempo" that sounds extreme but is probably typical for NSW units in the "sandbox." These operations have been hugely successful because SEALs have been able to develop their own intel—hopping on a helicopter, overflying a target location, taking photos—and then launching a mission based on this fresh, but perishable, information sometimes within a couple of hours of notification.

That tremendous agility paid off with the capture of enemy commanders like the Taliban's Mullah Khairullah Kahirkhawa in Paktika Province, Afghanistan, in February 2003. A Predator drone aircraft transmitted video showing the mullah leaving a building under surveillance. Danish special operations personnel and SEALs quickly loaded onto huge MH-53 Pave Low helicopters and were in the air in fifteen minutes. Ninety minutes after he left the building, the mullah was cuffed and captured.

SEALs are doing so many of these quick-reaction missions that the old planning cycle's meticulous preparation has sometimes been exchanged for a very rapid collection and mission design process. SEALs and the other personnel on these operations sometimes don't know much about the mission until they are briefed while the helicopters are en route to the target. While that trades some of the virtues of a careful plan for the virtues of fresh information, the results seem to validate the method in today's real-world direct-action missions.

"The World's Best Waterborne Warriors"—CPO Steven Bronson, Boat Guy (USN Retired)

"It bothers me that, whenever the news media shows naval special warfare boats in action, the caption normally calls them something like 'the SEAL boats.' Well, they are not the SEALs' boats; they are special warfare combatant craft and the guys who run them are professionals within the NSW community with their own independent missions and qualifications. Yes, we deliver SEAL squads to their objectives, but we do a lot of other things at the same time, often without any SEALs aboard.

"Captain Ray Smith drove this change after Desert Storm [Ray Smith would shortly become Rear Admiral Ray Smith]. He was dismayed at the loss of his combat-qualified and combat-experienced special boat sailors—these sailors were hard-working combat sailors, but almost immediately after Desert Storm, some ninety percent of those same sailors were transferred back to the fleet. Rear Admiral Ray Smith worked with Captain Tom 'The Hulk' Richards, commanding officer of Naval Special Warfare Center and initiated what would become the SWCC course, which graduates some of the world's best waterborne warriors. SWCC sailors are volunteers who choose to attend a selection course and a qualification course and finally receive orders to a special boat team.

"I was proud to be one of the original eight sailors who were assigned to develop, design, implement, and train sailors in the SWCC course. I was eventually assigned as the program manager of SWCC for almost three years. It was truly an intense training program, which has continued to improve to where they are today.

"The Zodiac F470 is still the boat of choice for a mission where you need to get some guys to the beach and into the hinterland. You can get eight combat-equipped men or up to about three thousand pounds of cargo and run it all onto a beach, then hide the boat, do your mission ashore, and exfiltrate undetected. You can drive two of them right up on the back of a Mark Five, and that makes it a unique platform for missions where multiple boats are required. The F470 is the operator's best friend when you need to put a small unit ashore covertly.

"The eleven-meter RIB is getting a tremendous workout for the offshore missions today. It is extremely fast and stable, has special seats that accommodate an eight-man squad of SEALs, and can be crewed by five to eight SWCC boat guys. When set up for a wartime load-out, these boats mount weapons fore and aft, with a crewman on each, plus a communicator, a navigator, and the guy who is driving the boat. This boat fits inside some military aircraft and can be delivered quickly to anywhere they are needed.

"We're all pleased with the performance of our fairly new riverine assault craft, the SOC-R. Although it isn't discussed much in public, we've got a lot of special operations forces guys doing counter-narcotics missions in Central and South America, and these boats are natural choices for patrolling the rivers and estuaries of these regions."

The New Boats

The broad, heavily armed SOC-R, which can carry a whole squad, is a thirty-three-foot boat with tremendous speed and agility, but it is not the only vehicle currently available to the SEALs and SWCC.

Two U.S. Navy SEALs navigate through murky waters during a Combat Swimmer Training dive. Although all of America's special operations forces receive scuba and other underwater training, SEALs are the world's foremost combat swimmers. *U.S. Navy photo by Senior Chief Mass Communication Specialist Andrew McKaskle*

Special Warfare Combatant-craft Crewmen (SWCC) transit the Salt River in northern Kentucky during pre-deployment, live-fire training. SWCCs attached to Special Boat Team (SBT) 22 based in Stennis, Mississippi, employ the Special Operations Craft Riverine (SOC-R), which is specifically designed for the clandestine insertion and extraction of U.S. Navy SEALs and other special operations forces along shallow waterways and open water environments. *U.S. Navy photo by Mass Communication Specialist 2nd Class Jayme Pastoric*

Since 1992, NSW forces have been using the Mk V extensively and successfully. The eighty-one-foot Mk Vs don't have the ability to operate independently for extended periods, but they are very fast, efficient, and capable. They've worked out well during combat operations in the Gulf, and both SEALs and the boat guys are generally pleased with them.

"The question," CPO Steven Bronson (USN ret.) says, "was why should SWCC use a 175-foot boat and a crew of twenty-five men when they can send two Mk Vs with a combined crew of ten men to do the same basic real-world mission? It just made much more sense to go with the Mark Vs."

In 1993, the first of fourteen *Cyclone*-class coastal patrol crafts (PCs) was commissioned to replace the aging sixty-five-foot Mk III patrol boats operated by NSW's special boat units. The primary mission of the PC was to conduct coastal patrol,

surveillance, and interdiction operations in support of NSW. The boats turned out to be excellent vessels and were well received by theatre commanders. Subsequent budgetary concerns resulted in the PCs being slated for decommissioning; however, in the wake of the 9/11 terrorist attacks, thirteen of the fourteen ships were turned over to the navy and employed overseas and in support of Operation Noble Eagle. The first PC commissioned, USS *Cyclone*, was transferred to the U.S. Coast Guard in 2000 and then transferred to the Philippines as BRP *Mariano Alvarez* (PS 38) in March 2004.

"The Weak Die Young"—Anonymous Former SEAL

"Being in the special operations community now, especially in the SEALs, is a very good experience. SEAL teams are

Plain Vanilla and Extra Crunchy— Life in the Teams Today

SEALs and guys on the Special Boat teams will tell you that there are essentially two kinds of SEAL teams today, the "plain vanilla" type and the one very special team, the one with the extra nuts and toppings. The special team is ST6, the plain vanilla teams are all the rest. "All the teams are well funded today," one member of the community says, "but SEAL Team Six has money for almost anything they ask for."

Wish You Were Here

Ten years of sustained combat operations have refined SPECWARCOM's business model in many ways. For one thing, when a team deploys now (2011), the whole unit packs up and heads downrange—the commander, the entire staff, the supply and support people, and the team members too. In the past, a lot of the command group stayed home and worked somewhat normal duty days, went to the bar after work, went home on weekends. No more—the whole unit deploys as a package deal. The SEALs have always been used to that, but for some of the support personnel and administrative staff, a "headspace" adjustment has been required.

Riggers

Among every unit that deploys are several important men who operate sewing machines instead of machine guns: the riggers. These guys are always available to customize uniforms and web gear, and they can fabricate bags, containers, slings, and anything else you might need to complete a mission. If you look closely at the shirts most SEALs wear, you will see small pockets on the upper sleeve area; these are added by the riggers under the direction of individual SEALs and SBS crewmen. An entire industry has evolved from the riggers and their custom sewing skills, the most successful of which is Blackhawk Industries, a company started by ex-SEAL Mike Noell to build bags and vests for tactical operators. Today there are dozens of companies like Blackhawk selling specialized gear for SEALs and other operators, designs that have evolved from the custom tailoring work of NSW riggers.

Guns and Gear

SEALs typically seem to have the most flexibility and choice of gear and weapons of all the units in the American armed forces. If anybody is going to have the option of acquiring a new rifle or radio, it's going to be the guys on the teams and especially the guys on SEAL Team Six.

Among those exotic rifles has been the SOF Combat Assault Rifle, or SCAR-H Mk 17 shown in the photograph on this page, a modular weapon built by FN Herstal and adopted by USSOCOM in 2003. Intended as an upgrade for the venerable M16/M4 platform in use since the mid-1960s, the 5.56mm version, the Mk 16 SCAR, was withdrawn from issue while the heavier 7.62mm SCAR-H and a sniper variant, the Mk 20, are currently being issued. This SEAL's Mk 17 is tricked out with a PEQ-15 target pointer and illuminator, fore-end grip and integral switch for the pointer, scope, and a bipod. The PEQ-15 is the latest generation (at

A U.S. Navy SEAL takes up a defensive position in a village in northern Zabul province, Afghanistan. *U.S. Navy photo by Chief Mass Communication Specialist Jeremy L. Wood*

this writing) of a whole family of night-fighting high-technology tools. It can provide broad-beam, overall illumination like a flashlight and a precise laser spot-targeting marker, both visible only to those wearing NODs (night observation devices).

One career senior petty officer says about SEALs and their gear, "There is a tremendous emphasis on fine-tuning everything a guy carries on an op. Weight is a huge factor and every ounce is considered. And although there's usually money for any kind of comm gear and beacons and all the other high-tech stuff, SEALs will generally prefer equipment that is powered by AA batteries if it's available. You can buy AA batteries anyplace in the world, from North Korea to any back street in Botswana, and that can be really important for a team on an operation."

Reach Out and Touch Somebody

Until fairly recently, the role of snipers throughout the American armed forces tended to emphasize covert observation from a distance with actual engagement of targets with their rifles being a secondary and somewhat rare mission. That has been changing radically in the past few years, and now snipers are now doing more killing, man for man, than is anybody else. SEAL snipers in particular have been busy with their rifles, sometimes providing support for U.S. Army and Marine Corps conventional infantry units far from the ocean.

The tools of the sniper's trade have improved along with the importance of the mission. SEAL snipers at this writing are using a wide variety of exotic and expensive sniper rifles—the SR-25, the SCAR-H, CheyTac, and others, usually with very powerful optics. While the army and Marine Corps snipers are still using rifles built around the 7.62mm NATO cartridge, good to about 800 meters on a normal day and 1,200 meters if you're really lucky, SEAL snipers are using weapons built around much heavier cartridges—.300 Winchester Magnum, .338 Lapuua, .375 CheyTac, and .408 Cheytac, all of which are effective to 1,500 meters and beyond. SEALs are also getting some extremely capable and expensive ballistic computer systems that enhance the chance of a first-round hit at extreme range.

Members of SEAL Delivery Vehicle Team Two (SDVT-2) prepare to launch one of the team's SEAL Delivery Vehicles (SDV) from the back of the Los Angeles–class attack submarine USS *Philadelphia* (SSN 690) on a training exercise. The SDVs are used to carry Navy SEALs from a submerged submarine to enemy targets while staying underwater and undetected. SDVT-2 is stationed at Naval Amphibious Base Little Creek, Virginia, and conducts operations throughout the Atlantic, Southern, and European command areas of responsibility. A contract for an advanced SEAL Delivery System (ASDS) was awarded in 1994. The ASDS could transport up to sixteen SEALs in a dry chamber, allowing much longer underwater missions than possible with the SDV. A total of six ASDSs were to be built. To date only one ASDS has been built, and it suffered major damage during a fire in November 2008, which Special Operations Command has chosen not to repair due to funding constraints. Technical and reliability issues with ASDS-1 and 400 percent cost overrun have caused the demise of this program for the time being. *U.S. Navy photo by Chief Photographer's Mate Andrew McKaskle*

doing a lot of great missions—interception of suspect vessels at sea, disrupting enemy supply lines, reconnaissance of enemy personnel, and even snatch-and-grab captures of enemy commanders. SEALs are protecting the Iraqi prime minister and other missions of great responsibility.

"Being in a small unit like a SEAL team, you forge extremely strong bonds with the guys. In any group where you have sixteen or so AAA-personalities, there are going to be strong opinions and lots of competition. Once in a while you might bump heads with somebody else; if you're going to be on a SEAL team, you need to have very thick skin in addition to all the other qualifications. Within the platoon or squad, everything you do will be subject to critique and criticism and it pays to take it all cheerfully. We play by 'big boy' rules on the teams, and if you do something stupid, you're expected to own up to it right away.

"The most-junior member of the platoon is normally designated the 'beermeister,' and it is his job to make a record of each dumb stunt anybody makes during an exercise or operation. Later, at an appropriate time, each one of those mistakes will cost the SEAL who made it a case of beer. The result is that the whole unit has a good time but at the same time the mistake is recalled to the embarrassment of the SEAL who made it and who will be expected to avoid doing it again. Anybody who can't take criticism from his teammates will get criticized for that too—it is considered a weakness. The weak die young on a SEAL team."

The President of the United States in the name of The Congress takes pride in presenting the MEDAL OF HONOR posthumously to

LIEUTENANT MICHAEL P. MURPHY
UNITED STATES NAVY

for service as set forth in the following

CITATION:

For conspicuous gallantry and intrepidity at the risk of his life above and beyond the call of duty as the Leader of a Special Reconnaissance Element with Naval Special Warfare Task Unit AFGHANISTAN on 27 and 28 June 2005. While leading a mission to locate a high-level anti-coalition militia leader, Lieutenant Murphy demonstrated extraordinary heroism in the face of grave danger in the vicinity of Asadabad, Konar Province, Afghanistan. On 28 June 2005, operating in an extremely rugged enemy-controlled area, Lieutenant Murphy's team was discovered by anti-coalition militia sympathizers, who revealed their position to Taliban fighters. As a result, between 30 and 40 enemy fighters besieged his four-member team. Demonstrating exceptional resolve, Lieutenant Murphy valiantly led his men in engaging the large enemy force. The ensuing fierce firefight resulted in numerous enemy casualties, as well as the wounding of all four members of the team. Ignoring his own wounds and demonstrating exceptional composure, Lieutenant Murphy continued to lead and encourage his men. When the primary communicator fell mortally wounded, Lieutenant Murphy repeatedly attempted to call for assistance for his beleaguered teammates. Realizing the impossibility of communicating in the extreme terrain, and in the face of almost certain death, he fought his way into open terrain to gain a better position to transmit a call. This deliberate, heroic act deprived him of cover, exposing him to direct enemy fire. Finally achieving contact with his headquarters, Lieutenant Murphy maintained his exposed position while he provided his location and requested immediate support for his team. In his final act of bravery, he continued to engage the enemy until he was mortally wounded, gallantly giving his life for his country and for the cause of freedom. By his selfless leadership, courageous actions, and extraordinary devotion to duty, Lieutenant Murphy reflected great credit upon himself and upheld the highest traditions of the United States Naval Service.

U.S. Navy

The President of the United States in the name of The Congress takes pride in presenting the MEDAL OF HONOR posthumously to

MASTER-AT-ARMS SECOND CLASS (SEA, AIR AND LAND)
MICHAEL A. MONSOOR
UNITED STATES NAVY

for service as set forth in the following

CITATION:

For conspicuous gallantry and intrepidity at the risk of his life above and beyond the call of duty while serving as Automatic Weapons Gunner for Naval Special Warfare Task Group Arabian Peninsula, in support of Operation IRAQI FREEDOM on 29 September 2006. As a member of a combined SEAL and Iraqi Army sniper overwatch element, tasked with providing early warning and stand-off protection from a rooftop in an insurgent-held sector of Ar Ramadi, Iraq, Petty Officer Monsoor distinguished himself by his exceptional bravery in the face of grave danger. In the early morning, insurgents prepared to execute a coordinated attack by reconnoitering the area around the element's position. Element snipers thwarted the enemy's initial attempt by eliminating two insurgents. The enemy continued to assault the element, engaging them with a rocket-propelled grenade and small arms fire. As enemy activity increased, Petty Officer Monsoor took position with his machine gun between two teammates on an outcropping of the roof. While the SEALs vigilantly watched for enemy activity, an insurgent threw a hand grenade from an unseen location, which bounced off Petty Officer Monsoor's chest and landed in front of him. Although only he could have escaped the blast, Petty Officer Monsoor chose instead to protect his teammates. Instantly and without regard for his own safety, he threw himself onto the grenade to absorb the force of the explosion with his body, saving the lives of his two teammates. By his undaunted courage, fighting spirit, and unwavering devotion to duty in the face of certain death, Petty Officer Monsoor gallantly gave his life for his country, thereby reflecting great credit upon himself and upholding the highest traditions of the United States Naval Service.

U.S. Navy

Index

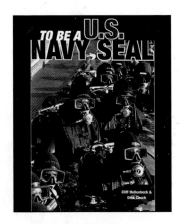

To Be a U.S. Navy SEAL
ISBN 978-0-7603-1404-3

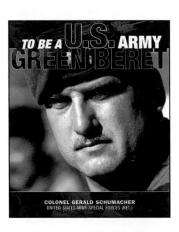

To Be a U.S. Army Green Beret
ISBN 978-0-7603-2107-2

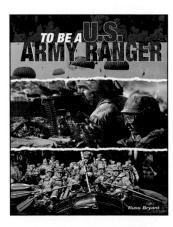

To Be a U.S. Army Ranger
ISBN 978-0-7603-1314-5

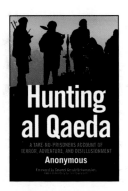

Hunting al Qaeda
ISBN 978-0-7603-3736-3

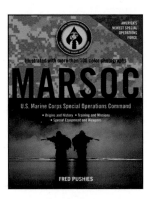

MARSOC
ISBN 978-0-7603-4074-5

Weapons of Delta Force
ISBN 978-0-7603-3824-7